REVAMP!

WHAT TO DO WHEN YOU DON'T KNOW WHAT TO DO

CHINWE EBERE A.

REVAMP! – What to do when you don't know what to do

ISBN: 978-978-970-778-2

Published by Chinwe Ebere A: https://linktr.ee/chinweandro

Dedication

First to God – Infinite Intelligence, who through the active contribution of the Sweet Holy Spirit gave me the wisdom to bring this to reality.

Then to my Parents, Siblings, Mentors, and Accountability Partners who never gave up on my dreams and built in me the zeal, faith and confidence to go all in and activate my greatest accomplishments.

I will also not fail to make mention of the team of Gathering of Extraordinary Female (GEF), whose invitation to speak at the 5.0 edition of the GEF gave rise to the topic **"Revamp"**.

Finally, to my first seed company, that presented the platform to really harness my potentials, **Andromagik Company** – a social enterprise dedicated to raising generations that are more self-aware, impact-driven, purposeful and future-focused, in the most innovative way.

CONTENTS:

AUTHOR'S PREFACE

On one faithful evening, at the point I had hit rock bottom after making an absolutely disruptive decision I knew was right at the time, but found difficult to accept because life wasn't looking like the "bread and butter" I had envisioned, I got an ah-ha moment that changed the trajectory of my entire life.

This moment didn't happen until I consciously moved past what looked like regrets, recognized the fact that I wasn't stranded, opened my mind to the potentials I had – a combination of my gifts, skills, talents, passions and experiences, and the enormous possibilities that was ahead of me if I could but link the bridges. Guess what? Few months down the line, I was sent an instagram direct message, "we'd like you to speak to our women", after which came the theme **REVAMP!**

It took me rethinking to realize that everything just aligned because I embraced my new reality, but with an open mind for what is to come. Although I fidgeted a second about "speaking", I forged ahead to begin my research on the theme, and slowly brought alive my experiences and that of everyone I had ever encountered.

On the D-day, I spoke only an abridged version of my research and knowledge, and this piece changed the lives of women and even men that attended. It was followed by calls for mentorships and finally a call back to speak on another theme in the same year.

Moving forward, I have expanded on my research and carefully put down personal experiences and those of families, colleagues, mentors, and accountability partners to birth this book I am positive will transform the trajectory of your life too. The most important thing I must advise is that the best way to use this book and have it work for you, is to pause when you should, reflect when you should, write when you should – literally do as stipulated throughout the book, leaving no pages unturned.

I pledge to follow you throughout the chapters and celebrate your milestones, as I look forward to your total **REVAMP**, the height you will attain by the conclusion of the chapters and continuous practice of the tasks, and the effortless victories ahead.

One last thing I must tell you is to GET A JOURNAL.

Your Partner in Success,

Chinwe Ebere A.

INTRODUCTION

Life is not a one way ride, if it was, there will probably be no failed attempts, limited resources, opportunity costs, difference in strategies and approaches to it, or the constant need to revamp, for the simple reason that one shoe will fit all. But one shoe can't fit all, can it?

This will mean that benchmarking your life based on someone else's achievements, limits, goals and strategies will fail in the long run. Fortunately enough, this multi-directional ride called life will give room for all your creativity to come to play, if properly harnessed and carefully managed. This, to me, sounds a lot better than focusing on living like everyone else or seeking validations from people, other than living your authentic life.

Authenticity reflects on how real you are from within – that point in your life where your needs, values, and actions, are accountable to what comes from within you and not an attempt to imitate or become someone the society, your conditioning, family or friends has forced on you. A life of authenticity is right at the centre of all genuine commitment to better yourself, overcome stagnation, and attain a life of satisfaction, all of which are subject to your ability to constantly **revamp!**

To revamp is to overhaul, change, regain relevance, match up expectations, stay ahead at all time, and rearrange an existing thing in order to seek ways to improve its previous performance or maintain your competitive advantage. The most successful individuals and organisations have come to the conscious or forced realization of the need to constantly revamp to fit in, or get ruled out of the equation of success in endeavors.

It is okay not to know what next to do, what isn't okay is not doing anything about it. So, whatever may, stay committed to becoming the best version of yourself, which finds its' root in the constant revamp of your life's strategies and approaches.

In progression, while some of these strategies and approaches might work for long term, some might only work for a limited time frame because of the dynamism of life, and others might fail from the get go as a result of the complexity change comes with. The influencing factors of these strategies and approaches go beyond the external – political, environmental, sociological, or technological, to those fragile internal factors we mostly ignore to address, like paradigms, mindsets, behaviors, and patterns, to mention but a few.

The victory of life comes from the awareness and assurance that as long as you refuse to get stuck in a futile strategy or complacence, you will find your life's fit, and as long as you keep revamping and improving, you will overcome stuck points, live satisfied, bask in fulfillment, and attain a life of authenticity.

When you don't know what to do, REVAMP!

REFLECTION EXERCISE

This reflection exercise will set the ball rolling...

On the 1st of January 2016, 100 people were given the keys and step by step guides on how to overcome stagnation, live in prolonged satisfaction, and finally attain success. After the first quarter, 15 people had effectively utilized the keys and secrets. However, by the 31st of December 2016, only 3 people had made evident progress.

With your own knowledge and in your own understanding, why did only 15 people utilize these keys and secrets?

____

____

____

____

____

____

____

Next, why do you think the number dropped from 15 to 3, and what happened to entire 97 that made no significant progress?

____

____

____

____

____

____

____

____

____

____

____

____

By the beginning of 2021, 5 years later, only 1 person became a true and evident definition of success.

What do you think happened to the other two who came thus far, but dropped on the way?

____

____

____

____

____

____

Finally, why did this "1 person" become successfully, and what did do you think he/she did differently?

____

____

____

____

____

____

____

____

____

____

____

____

It is so important that you reflect on this before you move on to the chapters ahead. Your responses will prepare you for the tasks ahead and see you through the completion of this book and all the in-betweens.

Note: No right or wrong answers. As you go through the chapters, you'd be able get more answers. You can review this again after you conclude with the book, and sincerely ask yourself "Am I the 99 or the 1?"...

SECTION 1: REDEFINING THE PATH

"The path to our destination is not always a straight one. We go down the wrong road, we get lost, and we turn back. Maybe it doesn't matter which road we embark on. Maybe what matters is that we embark."

— Barbara Hall.

WHAT DO YOU REALLY WANT?

*"If a man knows not to which port he sails,
no wind is favorable."*

— Seneca.

When the question of intended life outcome and the definition of satisfaction and fulfillment are asked to a good number of people, the majority of answers will focus on money, happiness, and perhaps peace too.

That's not such a bad idea, but becomes worrisome when one cannot further clarify what amount of money can translate to this immediate satisfaction, what this happiness and most sought after peace could mean in clearer and specific terms, to make it recognizable when it eventually happens. This means that it is possible amazing things are happening to you right now but are completely invisible to you, simply because they are not well defined.

The truth about why it seems difficult to see or take up opportunities that present themselves daily, move from stuck points, get true and long lasting satisfaction, is rooted in the inability to answer one of the most salient life questions:

- The "what" of desires – Precise definition of what we really want in all spheres of life.

Pause and Reflect: What do you really want from all major spheres of your life – relationship, marriage, career, business, finance, family, friends, recreation, and perhaps physical environment?

The foundation of the inability to define desires is that most lives are lived on "as the day goes by" basis – either just flowing with the present uncertainties or stuck on survival mode. Living an authentic life, and creating relevant impacts become impossible and difficult when the approach to life is lackadaisical, or the only focus is the need for "urgent 2k" - daily pennies for survival.

As a result of these approaches to life, lot of potentials are never discovered, dreams are not actualized, life changing innovations never become realities, and maximum satisfaction is never attained. It soon becomes a repeat cycle, as more and more generations come in and quickly adjust to the norm. No questions asked, many excuses given, and less concern about our individual role in the advancement of humanity.

In avoidance of this, it becomes crucial to know what you really desire, and answering this will help you decide your goal post - the destination, define expectations - for setting standards and making decisions, draft your roadmap - the strategies, design your methods - the navigation, and finally review your progress and outcomes - the measurement.

When you do answer this question, as it is recommended you do by the end of this chapter, you will see how closer you are to figuring out the ways to go, actualize your dreams, get good success and satisfaction, which will progressively come into physical evidences as God through the energies present in the universe, work them out for you, after you must have fulfilled your own part of the bargain.

It is critical to know however, that even with these clear and specific definitions, we cannot rule out the realities of changes in priority as you make progress and grow. These progress and growth could mean exceeding previous expectations, smashing all goals, but could also mean not meeting up to expectations - which is an opportunity to start again, smarter this time.

Goes without saying that what you want today might change tomorrow, or might need to be modified to fit into tomorrow's expectations. Here in lies the importance of flexibility to be able to revamp as often as possible.

DEFINE SPECIFICALLY

It is easier to spend the days screaming in everyone's ears about how successful you will become, how wealthy you will be, or even how undoubtedly perfect your next relationship will turn out. All valid and powerful envisioning until it is time to achieve these dreams of perfection or measure how far you have come with achievement, and you are totally clueless as to where to start measuring from.

So, define specifically...

Do you know your intended destination?

It is absolutely okay if you don't know at this point, but you really should by the conclusion of this chapter.

Crafting a destination is the foremost step to go, after all, would you wake up early every morning and set out to take a journey without knowing where you are going to?

Would you just turn on your car engine every day and start driving to just anywhere the "spirit" leads?

Truthfully, we cannot rule out the rare place of spontaneity in journeying. I have a good friend who has literally visited all the countries of the world, all, a good number of which were spontaneous travels. He could decide to get into one Country in West Africa, and the next thing, boredom drives him to other Countries.

Yet, even with traveling being his hobby, when he is set to achieve anything reasonable in a particular Country, he plans even more carefully. As it relates to life, you most definitely can't always leave your life to chance and ask yourself why things don't seem to be working out year in and year out.

Here's an illustration: Tess might decide that her destination is to become the first female governor in her state...

What are your expectations?

Knowing your destination is not enough to get you there! The first thing is your destination, and the next is what you expect would come out of it. A different height of impossibility is planning to achieve all the goals in the world without a clear definition of what an actual achievement is, in line with those goals.

The reason why there are visions, missions, core

values, and departmental standard of operation (SOPs) in businesses is so that asides from the initial designers knowing the expected future outcomes, everyone else who comes into the organisation has a unanimous focus. Individually, you need to draw up expectations so it is easy to set standards you shouldn't compromise, make decisions, form a basis for deriving numerous methods and strategies, and for measuring your progress.

Tess' expectation is that people will vote for her if she's able to win their hearts, so she begins early enough to set her life's vision, mission and values...

Are there strategies in place?

Why do you think organisations that record continuous successes draw up plans – marketing, business development, sales, human resources, administration, finances, operations, and all other departmental strategies for any new year? If you will get desired outcomes, you must decide the strategies that need to be put in place per time.

The uncertainties of tomorrow will never be enough excuse or reason not to set goals. As you have defined your destination, pin pointed your expected outcomes, you must put strategies in place for how to navigate, and yet be open to revamp those strategies.

Tess might then decide that two of out of all her strategies will be to go to the university and study a relevant program or get into grassroots politics...

What are your methods?

Ironically, most people who tend to have already envisioned their destination – a good relationship, a collaborative marriage, starting up a business, etc., cannot exactly spell out what they need to do to get to this destination.

I still maintain that growing up as an African child was one of the toughest task life handed over to me, it didn't look rewarding at the get go but today, I still get rewarded. If you grew up in a family like mine you will only know how to define your destination but no one hands you the techniques.

For one, I wanted good friendships and to be in a loving relationship, but no one hands you the opportunity to bring friends home, let alone introduce a relationship. Also, I grew up wanting to become a banker, but no one handed me the methods in terms of the course to study or what to do differently. But was that enough excuse not redesigning my techniques as I grew up? No!

Tess' navigation methods and techniques might be starting the course, networking more, identifying and initiating solutions to grassroots community problems, or perhaps registering and becoming an active political party member...

How would you review your progress?

Journeying to a destination will make no sense without checkpoints. In literal terms, checkpoints are "the points where checks are done", absence of which will result in a carefree ride that would constitute road nuisance.

Applying it to our context, "no life checkpoints" automatically translate to a rough destiny and purpose ride. That's like saying "oh, I'm heading to the position of the wealthiest person in my sphere of influence", yet stay oblivious of what it will take to get you there, and create checkpoints that will help in measuring your progress.

Now, Tess has put all other things to place, but that will never be complete if there are no ways to measure her performance in relations to her destination, expectation, strategies and navigation techniques...

Reflective Illustration:

Would you after deciding to make a mouthwatering meal, fail to think and define specifically, all the things you will need to purchase to achieve this?

When you define the details of what you will need, would it not be easier to tick off or cross out those things already purchased, and do the much to make sure everything needed is gotten before leaving the mall or supermarket as the case may be?

If so much specificity goes into a meal, how much more your life? How do you know that you have achieved a new height that takes you closer to your destination?

Reflection Exercise:

Ask yourself the following questions in deep reflection, for these nine (9) major areas of life – relationship and love, fun and recreation, business and career, family and friends, health and fitness, money and finances, personal growth, physical environment, and spiritual life:

- What do I really want from these spheres of my life?
- How can I define them in clear terms? *See example below.*
- What do I expect from each of these spheres of my life?
- Are there strategies I need to put in place?
- What am I willing to give up getting all I want?
- What am I willing to learn to get my desired outcome?
- At what point would I say I have achieved these things?

Example: For a relationship and love, ask:

If I want a perfect relationship and love, what does "perfect" mean? Is it any of the 5 love languages according to Dr. Gray Chapman– acts of service, receiving gifts, quality time, words of affirmation or physical touch? Is it financial security, if so, how much finances is security enough for you? Is it educational level, if so, what qualifications? Is it how you want to be treated? Saying you would love to be treated "nicely" is not specific, until you define what "nice" means to you... etc.

Apply the above to the other areas of life listed above, and then proceed to the next step.

THINK ON PAPER

You can only know yourself or desires when you must have thought them out, but actualizing them only happens when they are written on papers! Beyond the thoughts of them, have the hardcopy evidence of them.

Truth remains that whatever you do not write down becomes difficult, if not impossible to achieve. The human mind is constantly in a battle of what information should be domicile in it, with new regular distractions coming to take over the older ones. Ideas that are only stored in your head, quickly get replaced with the next sensational news on social media or even another idea.

There are so much that never gets done, and escalating number of unexplored potentials because people conceive great ideas and become multi billionaires out of these ideas, only in their HEADS and MINDS.

Experience has driven me to meet a lot of great minds, whose ideas have the capacity to give the entire world a total disruptive blessing, but they never get done, because while majority hate the idea of writing, minority would rather not write because they always misplace journals – such excuse!

Have you ever wondered why an idea that seems novel to you when conceived quickly becomes a new global sensation the next few months or years? This is because ideas are available for everyone and it works as such: Infinite Intelligence releases ideas freely to everyone whose purpose aligns with it, and who has the perceived mental capacity to accumulate those ideas. If you are ever able to think on paper and act almost immediately, you gain the first mover advantage.

The above illustration is only a little importance of thinking on paper. When you have defined specifically, think them out on paper. Thinking on paper will save you the consequences of going in the circle of confusion, give you an edge as long as you act fast, and it also serves as a great way of self-accountability and progress assessment.

What to do?

All of those earlier questions you reflected on should now come on papers if they haven't already. Yes, having phone note pads are good but having physical journals are even better. Get a bedside journal and a pocket/purse note to be with you throughout the day. Your phone note pad can be used in place of pocket/purse notes depending on your present location and activity.

Having these will help you capture eureka moments at every time of the day. Eureka moments are those "aha" moments when answers come unexpectedly in form of ideas, nudges or solutions, and it mean exactly as named, "ah ha"! And if you miss out on capturing an "ah ha" moment, it might never come again and if it does, it might take a while. Why wait?

CREATE YOUR BIG PICTURE

Now you have succeeded in defining what you want in specific terms and in various spheres, it is important to create the big picture for each of them. What is this big picture and why is it important?

Some time ago during the writing of this great book, I had a conversation with one of the most amazing human push life blessed me with, after which she asked me a question "how would you know you have made it?" Ironically, earlier on the same day, a mentee asked me the same question. I knew the universe needed me to respond to that question.

Without a big picture, answers to this question might never come. Permit me to throw you into another deep reflection...

Dear Friend and Reader, How would you know you have made it?

Having a clearly defined destination doesn't mean you can see a big picture - your success evidence.

The absolute truth about big pictures is that you have got to see the future, before you see the future - you must get there in your mind before your body ever gets there. I am not speaking about day dreaming endlessly without making an attempt to get there, but dreaming, bothering less about how to get there, and still making conscious efforts to get there.

Visualizing your big picture

If you walk into my office or my house space, you will see photos and write ups that depict what I want my reality to be. Before now I had vague ideas of what I wanted for my future until I learned the "law of attraction" some years ago, that emphasizes that if you hold a thought for so long, you quickly bring it into your reality. I tried it countlessly, it worked for every time, and I eventually made a habit of it.

Pause and reflect: Why do you think when you tell yourself you want a particular car, the moment you step out you start seeing it everywhere? Now that is the power of attracting your thoughts.

Likewise, if you see a picture of a future you want for so long, you feed that into your subconscious mind which emits same into the universe as energies, that eventually become your reality *(A little more focus on this in the next chapter)*.

Based on diverse experiences and my findings, I have come to realize that there are basically four things you attract to yourselves:

- Your mindset: Your most dominant thoughts – good or bad.

- Your purpose targets: Those who you have been destined to impact on.

- Your insecurities: If for instance you think so low of your appearance, you attract people who affirm that.

- Your reflection: Who you see when you look into the mirror.

If you see abundance, you get it, eventually. If it's lack you see, the universe won't stop you from having it either.

What to do?

Create a vision board (Pictorial representation of the big picture.) Browse the internet and download pictures that represent the kind of life you want to live. Download pictures of houses, offices, teams, people, global meetings, marriages, buildings, cars, audiences, congregations, meetings, aged people who are healthy, food types, etc. that depicts the kind of life that you want to live.

Note that this will differ one to another... if you don't intend speaking or singing to a crowd or any career similar, getting an audience might not be necessary for you. Let your picture show the life you want, not anyone else's or the life someone wants for you.

WHY "HOW TO GET THERE" SHOULDN'T BE YOUR CONCERN!

I recall words from one of my mentors, Bob Proctor of blessed memories:

The only thing to ask yourself when you set out to achieve a goal is "Do I really want it?" Forget the how! All the resources you need will come to you from wherever they are now.

Judging from the obvious realities we are surrounded by, at a stuck point, it is difficult to allow one's self create or dream about any big picture. We get worried about how the environment wouldn't let us become, how the world is too complex, the rate at which lives are disrupted, and every other thing in between, that we refuse to dream beyond that. Bothering about "how" to get what you really want has a unique way of crippling any potential attempt, simply because it gets so overwhelming for a common man.

Whoever watches the weather will never sow because there will never be a perfect time to sow. If you put so much efforts on how to get there, getting there will not happen because questions on "how" shifts you to actively consider all the limiting factors and forces that will continually be present.

Your business is to know what you want, have the big pictures for it, and start doing what it takes to get there. Some of which will include bettering yourself, adjusting habits, changing routines, eating healthier, switching career paths, and rebuilding your values. Once you start moving at all, you automatically begin to attract the right connections, ideas, networks, career path, etc.

SET GOALS, BREAK THEM INTO BITS

You have a defined destination now, while the universe sorts out how and the links on getting there, the part of setting goals belongs to you. Setting goals defer from dreaming or carving out big pictures because while dreaming might be unrealistic to the human comprehension, goal setting must be in a HEART format:

- **H**onest in its fit with your ambitions and aspiration.
- **E**xact in specific and precise steps you will need to take.
- **A**uthentic in line with your values and alignment with what you really want.
- **R**ealistic in whether you will truly have a consistent energy and motivation to commit to its' achievement.
- **T**imely in terms of checkpoints and deadlines.

Here is a detailed example of the thin line between dreaming and setting goals:

One Big Dream: I want to build a village of possibilities where the skills of various impaired people will be built and harnessed for global relevance, hereby eradicating the bias and number of impaired underserved pleading for alms on major cities of the world.

Goal Setting: If I need to get to my big dream, I will first need to have an idea of the statistics of impaired people in the world, perhaps how they got impaired, the possible skills that will make them relevant, if I cannot learn those skills, where can I connect with people who have them... the courses I will need to take – emotional intelligence, social care, etc., the company or foundation I will need to create, who I will need to mirror to learn how to create and scale them... how many times a day I need to do this... how will I measure my performance daily, weekly, monthly and annually... etc.

How the bridge between your dreams and goal setting will be linked:

While you are busy setting and smashing your daily, weekly, monthly and annual goals in consistency and without relenting or staying down after a fall, God through the active energies present in the universe, seeing how serious you are, will begin to link you to the relationships you will need to build, that mentor you will need to mirror, the course you'd have to take, that problem you will have an idea to solve... on and on, until the big picture starts to form, and boom! You have built that village of possibilities! Hurray!

CHAPTER RECAP

10 key things to remember from this chapter

1. There is no limit to how far you can go if you know and define your desires in clear and precise terms.
2. Every area of your life is equally important. Do not define some and leave out the rest.
3. Having it in your head is not enough to bring it into materialization; you need to think on paper.
4. It is important to have a way to measure your success and this is what defining helps you to achieve.
5. Eureka moments happen all the time in form of ideas, solutions, nudges, and instructions, but leave almost as soon as they come, so be swift to capture them.
6. Your vision board is a pictorial representation of all you want. Get them printed and paste it where you can see them every day.
7. You attract your mindset, purpose targets, insecurities, and reflection.
8. How to get to your desired outcomes is not your duty to worry about. Your duty is to design your outcome, set goals, be diligent about your journey, and have faith.
9. Goal setting shifts your mind from the "how" question, gets your mind off the present realities, and help you overcome how overwhelming the big picture gets.
10. When you create your big picture and start setting goals towards achievement, the universe produces the how and create the links in form of connections, ideas, wisdom, etc. to get to your big picture.

CHAPTER EXERCISE

Complete this in your personal journal.

Flip to the centre of your journal and write a heading "MY 100". Now, create a list of 100 things you want to achieve before kicking the bucket, assuming there's an addition of 50 years to your current age.

This 100 should cover all areas/spheres of your life, and in creating it, don't worry about being realistic to the human mind, whatever you can think about, you can be about it and can actualize. This 100 will also form the basis for setting personal goals.

Note this: Do not be pressured to complete your 100 in one sitting, this could take you months or maybe years, but make sure you keep progressing and keep ticking out as you achieve.

Your Special Treat!

After you complete this chapter, including the reflection and exercises, grab a box of chocolate! Hurray! I join you in celebrating your progress!

WHAT IS STOPPING YOU?

"Nothing can stop you until you choose to be stopped."

— Robin S. Sharma.

Most people know the height they aspire to attain, and if you have completed the previous chapter successfully, chances are you now do. One way or the other, you will begin to engross yourself with thinking and daydreaming about these things, maybe a little more than what a thought could reasonably handle. More times than never, the problem is actually getting there; sadly, even attempts to take baby steps look so difficult to do. Why?

Why should a well-orchestrated dream be so difficult to bring to reality? Stoppers!

As the name implies, they stop one, belittle the progress of the other, and reduce the efforts and enthusiasm of another, until they get to the break point of not making any attempt to actualize those dreams already identified. A dream remains a dream until we take the time to identify those forces stopping us now, or with the potential to stop us as soon as we start taking actions and making progress, or after a fall.

We all have stoppers, but the victory is identifying, becoming self-aware of the most common stoppers, and working towards consciously eradicating them, or reducing them to the most insignificant point. This being said, never feel weird being at a place of confusion or stagnation caused by stoppers, because everyone has a stopper or two from time to time.

Although it is a huge step successfully identifying and defining in clear terms, what you want out of life, it is yet another effort to start moving towards the actualization, and these effort can be rendered mere if you do not address your stoppers.

Stoppers could either be external or internal, but while a huge chunk of this is pointed to the unfavorable external environment, when we begin to look inward, we will understand that every individual possess them, consciously or unconsciously. Our key focus is on the internal stoppers which have more destructive tendencies than those externally influenced. They are literally those habits, mindset, experiences, and other frequently occurring events that prevent us from getting to the apogee of life.

While external stoppers are those political, economic, social, technological, legal and environmental (PESTLE) factors we could never influence from the comfort of our keypads and phones at home, internal stoppers make one suffer for what might or most times, might not exist.

It is one weird reality that a lot of people go through life suffering imaginarily – self created suffering through imaginations.

When you must have set out to design life goals, make a self-assessment of what stopped you, is currently stopping you, or what has the potential of stopping you when you begin journeying, or for every time you hit a mental roadblock in the course of your journey. Do you know your stoppers? It will amaze you at how much you become able to control them by simply becoming aware of them.

For this chapter, I have categorized these stoppers into the past, the present and the future – five sub-focuses in all:

THE PAST

These are blasts from things that happened to us in the past – a one time or repetitive pattern, a hurt or failure we have stubbornly refused to let go of, or worse, a circumstance that befell someone we know, but we have unconsciously picked as our own reality and are paying the price for something without an evidence of truth – even with an evidence, we are clueless of the event that created that circumstance. I've discussed two critical past stoppers below:

PARADIGM

The human mind is divided into the conscious and sub-conscious mind (further discussed in **the magic of the mindset**). While the conscious mind is a collection of things we carefully or carelessly feed in through our five sense organs, the sub-conscious mind is a build up from the effect of those things we took in through our conscious mind – the root of every blessing or curse.

As toddlers, we lacked the capacity to think for ourselves, as such, every caretaker that raised us, every society and environment we grew up in, or institution we attended, successfully fed into us all manner of beliefs that don't initially belong to us.

Most times, we play out roles that are not originally

ours but was created for us, rather than what we consciously created for ourselves. Our paradigm is seen in various aspects of our lives and the way you judge these aspects.

For instance, paradigm is seen in most common belief of the roles men and women are designed to play – you hear statements like "men don't cry" or "women belong permanently in the kitchen"; it is seen in those specific courses we grew up believing were the only worthy courses – medicine, law and banking; it is seen in the arguments about what an ideal relationship is or isn't; it is seen in our conclusion that failure is the roadmap to success, and in other spheres of our lives.

A repetitive example of a paradigm that has created toxicity in today's world is when two best friends' starts acting like strangers the moment they become "husband" and "wife", because of unhealthy expectations that has been crafted into their minds by the society and the key players in their upbringings, of characters a husband or wife should possess.

Pause and reflect: When was the last time you did something because you wanted to, and not because someone else compelled you to?

The magic of the mindset explains further and guides you on how to overcome the wrong mindsets created by paradigms.

What to do?

Make a list of all your caregivers or key influencers to your upbringing, write out the roles they played that you are currently playing. Is it your thought on suffering before succeeding? Letting go of relationships without proper communication? Whatever it is, how well is it serving you now? If it isn't, it is time to kick it all out and take your power back!

In your journal, make a list of your identified paradigms in precise words. Tick off those that aren't serving you anymore – those that has caused you repeated fails or caused so many complaints from those closest to you. Now, write what you want your life to be in those areas.

The Magic of the Mindset

The mind is the most powerful entity ever designed for man, where he can create, destroy, breakdown, rebuild, heal, and fix his life and any other thing that is within or even outside his immediate reach. Sadly, only a handful of people utilize this powerful entity for the positive.

It is my point of reemphasis on this singular fact that nothing happens in our lives that had not previously happened in our minds, except those very few unexpected outcomes. The mind is that creative force that singles you out from the crowd or makes you just like the mass – the same that distinguishes between the affluent few (1% of the 1%) on one side, and the mass on the other extreme side of life's spectra.

Indeed there are two sides to the coin of life, the thoughts or conceptualization and the manifestations or reality, controlled by the conscious and the subconscious mind respectively. The conscious mind uses the five (5) sense organs to pick signals, meaning it feeds on things seen, heard, felt, said or tasted, but the subconscious mind on the other hand, respectfully and obediently picks up signal from the conscious mind and emits the same to the universe in form of energies, which in turn gives us what we desire, knowingly or unknowingly, negative or positive, *eventually.*

The conscious mind can be controlled with efforts, through affirmations, positive self-talks and autosuggestion, and fed into the subconscious mind, because it works on instructions received from the conscious mind. There is a strong interconnectivity between both.

Note that the subconscious mind does not know what is right or wrong, and therefore can be "tricked" into believing that life is perfect if you control your conscious mind to utilize your sense organs for only positive things that affirms positivity.

For instance, with the roaring economy, if you suggest to your conscious mind that life is perfect for you, the subconscious mind picks "perfect" and sends straight to the universe, and you soon start seeing perfection amidst the economy turbulences. The beauty of this is that sooner than you imagine, the universe gives you that "perfection", and even when every other person is struggling to survive, life becomes untraceably interesting for you. There is a need to master the mind!

The mind as the first point of reference to physical evidences and outcomes will play out nothing different from what has been fed in. Invariably, every battle won in the mind can be replicated in the physical.

Pause and reflect: How much power do you have? How much have you allowed your external environment and present situations to control? We all have voices in our head, what do you do about yours?

What to do?

Give your mindset a name and treat it as a human being, become aware of when it speaks to you, when it tells you something negative, when it tells you something cannot be achieved, and know when to tell it to keep **shut.**

Create an affirmation list against your most dominant mindset, read continuously till it becomes a habit and finally your reality. For instance, if you grew up learning that you must struggle to survive, then create an affirmation that says: "I achieve my goal with ease" or "Everything comes easy for me, I just need to do my best and I get blessed instantly", etc.

Place your affirmation somewhere you can see it every day! For me, I have them on my phone, in my office, and around my apartment. Read it as often as possible, until your subconscious mind begins to accept it and starts emitting same.

UNFORGIVENESS

When ranking becomes necessary, unforgiveness will take a spot as the second major stopper, after the mindset. We deal so unjustly with ourselves and others, so much that we are unable to move from a mentally limiting spot even when we know these limits are caused by grudges we have refused to let go of.

Most people say forgiveness is probably the hardest and most difficult adjective in the English dictionary to practice. On a really light note, I find it quite hilarious; never to belittle this somewhat public opinion, but come to think of it, do have you not thought that things are only as hard and difficult as we say they are?

"True justice is paying once for each mistake. True injustice is paying more than once. Animals pay once, humans pay thousands of time. Every time we remember, we judge ourselves and feel guilt over and over again"

— Edgar Cayce

Moving beyond our past unpleasant experiences is incomplete without forgiveness, and as it is important to forgive past hurts from people you had probably trusted with your life, the forgiveness of self is considerably twice as important, because you can never give out what you don't already have. Forgiving others is not possible if you haven't already forgiven yourself. You've got to decide to stop paying for your mistakes over and over again.

Here are 5 things to do if you are constantly struggling with forgiveness and letting go of past hurts:

1. **Awareness and Acceptance:** The first step to solving any problem is becoming aware that there is a problem. This begins with an acceptance that they really did hurt you, a willingness to regain your power, and finally become free from their effect. If you think about them, what was done to you, or something you see triggers fresh feelings of rage or disappointment, it is an indication you need to heal from it.

   Fact: Running away or playing tough does not heal the wound, it only keeps it for the next potential victims. It goes on and on, until it eventually becomes a pattern and hinders the future. You surely don't want that...

2. **Forgive yourself first:** This step is more important than forgiving them because it is impossible to give what you don't have. Like it is generally said, it is impossible to love someone else, if we don't first love ourselves. This also applies to forgiveness. In what way have you been blaming yourself for what they or you did? NO MORE! Quit blaming yourself, you really didn't know better some years ago but now you do. So, forgive yourself for that knowledge gap.

   Tip: Affirm to yourself in these exact words: I am better than I was years back. I have no guilt or shame regarding what happened to me. I now know better and I am doing better. I release myself of every blame regarding ______________ (insert what you blame yourself about). Read this as often as possible, until your subconscious mind accepts it and starts living in the reality of it.

3. **Consciously forgive them:** After you have forgiven yourself, find closure. Finding closure means talking about that hurt created. "Talking" in this sense could mean talking to the right person, preferably a happiness coach, writing your offenders a letter, an email or a text.

   Tip: You could decide to show them, call them or **not**. That is solely up to you but should not affect your result. Importantly, if you decide to reach out to them, never attach your result to their responses. They might never be sorry for what they did, but that shouldn't bother you. What matters is the happiness and satisfaction you derive from knowing that the baggage is gone!

4. **Count your blessings, pick the lessons:** Every downside of life is a potential blessing. Most times, all you need to really do is look at it from a different perspective. You do know that "6" to a person on the left hand side, might be "9" to someone on the right. If you look closely, you will find your answers and when you do, be grateful for them. So here are common questions to ask:

   Questions: What did I learn? How has it made me

better? Did it teach me to treat others better? Was I saved from a future destruction? Would it have hindered me from living the life I am living now? If you can think, you can surely thank!

5. **Reinvent the wheel:** One of the most important things to do is identify those hurts that have become a repetitive pattern, those hurts that happen every time with different people. Could it be you have been compromising your standards all the while because you are scared no one else will accept you? Or you just haven't clearly defined a standard? You need to break the cycle and reinvent the wheel!

Tip: Have a detailed understanding of what you want based on instructions from chapter 1, what you are willing to accept, what you can no longer accept and define your expectations from friendships, relationships, career, and all other aspects of your life.

THE PRESENT

There are things we do today that have the capacity to hinder us from living the life of our dreams. At the thought of this, the first few things that will come to mind are procrastination, bad habits, the wrong circle, etc. While these are valid, if we look closer enough we'd come to realize that there are those very silent present stoppers that are not so evident, but can cause more harm than those listed above. I've discussed two critical present stoppers below:

PRESENT COMFORT

I recall critical conversations I have had with some people during my coaching sessions. One of the most striking was a conversation with a young man who had practically lost everything at the time, and had moved from a life where he got all he wanted, to a life where he had to struggle tirelessly to feed, yet with little or no result to show for the struggle.

When we met and he told me his story during his 30 minutes free consultation, I was moved to give him some probono sessions. Your guess is as good as mine, he couldn't keep up because for one, the tasks coaching comes with was too much a sacrifice, and secondly, he wasn't ready to come "all the way" to me.

It is easy to stay complacent or lay back when you are able to provide your daily meal and even a lot easier when you have tried all you can, but life doesn't seem to be responding as quickly as you expect. Does that sound familiar? Here's why: At the point where it feels like nothing is working despite all your efforts, you are pushed to stop trying, I mean, what's the point of trying right? The temptation to just live life as it comes becomes difficult not to succumb, and this is the worse place to ever be.

Be sure not to mistaken being contented with being "in comfort". In contentment, you are aware you are not where you should be at the time, yet you are grateful and happy, not envious of or trying to be like anyone else.

However, you are making daily efforts to get to the point of your desire. In present comfort, the focus drifts from gratitude and happiness to complains, yet with the unwillingness to go the extra mile to change anything.

Before you move on, I need you to understand that there is no way in the world that:

1. Your best is in the past.
2. Who you are is all you can be or are capable.
3. Where you are right now can be compared to where you can get to.

You were created as a potential and not as finality
— Yemi Davids,
Lead Pastor, Global Impact Ministries

The above statement formed part of what reconfirmed my ideology of all that I am capable, and sometimes I wish we can all sit back and really imagine the endless potentials we are.

Something striking happened to me during our support group's gratitude month in August 2021. The exercise was simple: "every day of the month, make a list of things you are grateful for". This exercise made me understand the importance of gratitude on one hand, and the many possibilities we are endowed with.

On one of the days, I looked around my apartment and smiled as I picked out the weirdest gratitude - the bulb, fan, washing machine, refrigerator, window, plates and everything around me. I was so excited, as I imagined the manner of thoughts that crossed the minds of those that invented these things, how they were able to make meaning out of it from raw materials into finished products.

Pause and reflect: Would it have been possible to create all of these things if they stayed stuck on present realities and their comfort zone?

Consider "playing" with this illustration before moving further: Shut your eyes for a bit and imagine the beauty of a tree, now I need you to task your mind and think out all the wonderful things that can be created from a tree:

An example from me: Furniture ☺

Now, your turn: ______________________________

____

____

____

____

____

____

____

____

____

____

If a non-living object can be converted into various finalities, how much more can you? I mean, you are Infinite Intelligence's greatest form of creation! Does the thought not make you excited!? If it does, as I hope it will, then it's time to get out of that comfort zone!

INGRATITUDE

We spend so much time complaining about what we do not have, what is not working at the time, and what should or should not be, that we forget what we have until we lose it all, and what we have becomes what we had, while what works turns into what used to work.

That is exactly what ingratitude does, steal it all away, and keep anyone in a stuck point and feeling of dissatisfaction for the longest time. Would you after gathering so much let it get stolen because you fail to give thanks?

The truth remains that if we take the time out to really reflect on our life's journey, we will come to realize that there is always something to be grateful for. Even the seemingly little things we take for granted are someone else's earnest prayer point and deepest desire. While you lament, get angry, or cry yourself to sleep over things that are not working as you have planned it, consider the following statements:

"If you do not have the mansion of your dream, at least you have a roof over your head. If you still do not have a roof over your head, you have a life you are not battling for. If you get so worried about the second degrees you are unable to bag, recall that a lot of other people could not even get a first degree. And if you are ashamed of not getting a first degree, remember that someone somewhere is bedridden and would give whatever it takes to be able to as little as socialize".

— Chinwe Ebere A.

There is always something to be grateful for. Think... Thank...

Should you ever think you have the worse life situation, take time out to watch the news, take a walk to the next street, visit a rehabilitation centre, have an excursion to the prison, or check out on displaced families. Not given to mockery of what anyone goes through, lest it becomes your reality, but for an in-depth understanding of why you should never take gratitude lightly.

A general misconception is that being too grateful might make you put less efforts to get to your next level. Understand this day that gratitude does not mean being satisfied with just a little; gratitude is not an excuse for slothfulness. On the contrary, gratitude is a push to even do more.

As you keep going in consistency, building the right success habits, working hard and smart, remember to celebrate your wins, and appreciate your progress.

Celebrating your wins, no matter how small and being grateful for all steps you take, has a way of feeding your mind with dopamine - feel good hormones. Feeling good has a positive effect on your mind, and that's an automatic suggestion to the universe to give you more of what you feel good about.

What to do?

Create three column gratitude lists.

One should focus on what you have enjoyed in the time past. The second should focus on what you currently enjoy out of life. The third should focus on your future - the desired future. As an instance, there's possibly an event that happened in the past, maybe an admission, a baby, or perhaps an accident you survived. If you intend to save the world, the third should state how grateful you are to be among the select few that will change the world.

After writing them all out, paste your gratitude list somewhere you can see it always and make a habit out of reading it as oft as possible.

Another interesting thing to do is choose a month in the year to make a gratitude month (Mine remains August). And for each day, you write down things you are grateful for - something that happened to you, something around you, or right about anything. Maybe the blue sky, a colorful bulb, a beautiful animal, anything.

THE FUTURE

When you look at the future from the eyes of a common man, there is the presence of fear of what it holds, doubt of what you carry, and anxiety of how to bridge the gap between where you are and want to get to. It is my most important emphasis that the future isn't yours to worry about, especially because in as much as you can do all it takes to prepare you for it, you cannot completely predict how it will go.

Regardless, your inability to predict the future outcome should never amount to "worrying about it", lest you unconsciously place a restrain on your abilities, or "flowing with the tides", lest you singlehandedly ruin its prospect *(Chapter 6 on live the moment expands this further)*. I've briefly discussed the most critical future stopper below:

FEAR

There is no doubt that we all have that one thing we are scared of, or are unwilling to try because we dread a possibly wrong and unfavorable outcome. But if you don't try, how would you really know?

I have so many first times, we all do – when we walked as toddlers, went to school for the first time, initially got married, had the first child, got the first job, spoke to a crowd for the first time, and the list goes on and on. When you look closely, you'd realize how much you dreaded that first time but eventually did it and it became the new best thing that happened to you.

While addressing the subject on fear, Napoleon Hill, author of "Think and grow rich", pointed out the most common – fear of failure, ill-health, poverty, criticism, loss of love, old age and death, but emphasized the need to focus less on the object of fear.

This is most crucial because consciously or unconsciously, like the phrase "energy goes where thought abides", sooner or later, you begin to attract what you focus so much energy on, and fear isn't an exception.

Pause and reflect: Do you ever wonder why the moment people are diagnosed with an ailment, it's almost like the symptoms increases and the ailment begins to skyrocket? Fear! If this isn't addressed intentionally, people end up dying because of the fear of the ailment and not the ailment itself.

You might have a lot to offer to the growth and betterment of humanity – we all do, but would the world ever feel it? How would you even try when all you are scared of is what people will say, and worry about being criticized for dreaming crazily or thinking differently?

If no one approves your dreams, do you approve it?

Maybe after much struggle and daily toils, your caregivers barely earned a living; as a result, you don't even try because you are scared you'd also end up in poverty... Does this sound familiar? Then know this day that we all have differing fate, and your success is up to you, and not tied to the same fate that befell that person.

During my first international podcast, a lady asked me a question and I'd reiterate in a closer rephrase: "I have a business idea but I am scared of starting, because I fear that I will fail". My response was simple "go to the direction of your fear". We never neglect the importance of preparation, but after that, do what you are scared of.

The problem is that our inquisition drives us to find more evidences to solidify those fears. How can you fear death, and focus only on the growing mortality rate? Or fear poverty, and focus on the increase in unemployment? What is the point of feeding yourself with failed marriages when you're afraid of losing love?

If you will ever overcome fear, find tangible reasons to counter it, and not more reasons to believe it.

What to do?

If fear and anxiety seems to easily grip you, look for someone who's fearless or evidence against the object of anxiety, and avoid people who fuels it.

If you are pregnant but fear child birth, rather than

find videos that increase the fear, find those with mothers that gave birth successfully. If you fear starting a business, avoid reading too much on the sky rocked failure rate of businesses, and find out how the successful people started theirs and watch out for the mistakes to avoid too...

CHAPTER RECAP

10 key things to remember from this chapter

1. No matter how well you define or design your expected outcome, stoppers have the potential of hindering its' manifestation.

2. Stoppers are present in everyone, but an earlier notice through self-awareness and sincerity will help you over power them.

3. There are external stoppers we have no direct control over, but the internal stoppers have more destructive tendencies. Deal with them.

4. You were created as a potential, not as finality. There are a lot you can still achieve.

5. Paradigms are stoppers from the past. They are those habits and mindsets we picked while growing up, and that has influenced our judgments and views about what life is or should be.

6. Unforgiveness is a strong stopper from the blasts of the past. You need to become aware, forgive yourself, forgive the offenders, pick out the blessings, and then reinvent the wheel.

7. If you stay too long in a particular situation, you are bound to become too comfortable, even when the situation isn't favorable.

8. Ingratitude, a present stopper can make you focus on what you don't have or isn't working until you lose what you already have or what is working.

9. The most common fears are fear of failure, ill-health, poverty, criticism, loss of love, old age and death. As a future stopper, fear can cripple your ability to try.

10. Get rid of anxiety. The future is yours to dominate if you do your best and leave the rest. But, always believe you can.

CHAPTER EXERCISE

Complete this in your personal journal.

With your understanding of what stoppers are, make a list of those things that had stopped you or gotten you to stuck points. How did they stop you or are stopping you now? For each, give a brief account of what happened.

With the understanding you now have, how do you think you can overpower it?

Your Special Treat!

After you complete this chapter, including the reflection and exercises, get yourself a new item! Bravo! I celebrate your progress with you!

CLOSE THE CRACKS, BRIDGE THE GAP

"One small crack doesn't mean that you are broken, it means that you were put to the test and you didn't fall apart."

— Linda Poindexter.

Once you have finally defined and designed all you want to achieve in major spheres of your life, and identified what had previously stopped you, and have the potential to stop you now or in the future, it is key to pick them out and close up the cracks that those stoppers - paradigms, hurts, mindset, unforgiveness, etc. had created in your life. After which you build a bridge that links those spheres together and finally to the grander picture.

Here's a practical view: Picture an old wall with weak concretes and cracks on them. If you can get this picture rightly, then you understand that with each seemingly minor crack comes the possibility of the wall cracking even further, harboring all manner of dangerous crawling animals and insects, and eventually falling apart if not attended to. This is exactly how life works.

Avoid further cracks

A further crack in the wall will continue to expand until it eventually affects areas that weren't previously affected. In our lives, this shows the potential of 1 stopper in an aspect of our life to grow into 2 stoppers, then 5, until it goes beyond 1 aspect of our life and into other aspects.

For instance, paradigms and hurts from childhood could begin to affect your relationship with your Significant other, family and friends, and then unforgiveness begins to creep in, and in no time comfort and ingratitude comes in, finally the fear and doubt about the future shows up.

Imagine what the nearest future will be when unaddressed relationships begin to affect your mental and physical health, and then finances will get affected because you need to pay for treatments, and the cycle goes on and on.

Give no room to harbor danger

If you look closely, those old cracks on the wall, especially those exposed soon become home to all manner of dangerous animals like reptiles and insects. Of course you know what happens when you least expect, these animals attack!

In our lives, this shows the potential of unaddressed stoppers to eat so deep they become dangerous habits that can cause loss of opportunities, relationships, or worse case, loss of the sense of self, even while alive.

Save it from falling apart

The finality of an abandoned crack on the wall which has been expanded beyond control is that it becomes so weak and finally gives way - fall. The danger of this might not be about the cost you will now incur in rebuilding, but worse off, what and who the wall falls on - further damages.

Our lives are no different, when you see dysfunctionalities moving from one generation to the other, characterized by increase in failed families, loss of empathy for humanity, skyrocketed crime rates, violence, and a diminishing society, a trace back could show you a wall whose crack was left untended to, until it fell.

In practice, life is a series of multiple connections and this implies that your spirituality is connected to your health, which is connected to your finances, which is connected to your career/business, also linked with your physical environment, and to your relationships (Significant other, family and friends). As such, you cannot afford to focus on an aspect and ignore the others, because what you ignore has the capacity of damaging what you didn't.

CLOSE THE CRACKS

Never blame yourself for the times you didn't know about these stoppers. If you successfully completed chapter 2 exercises, chances are that you are on the right track and now aware of them. Although there is that tendency of not addressing them completely at once, but with sincerity, a careful thought and repeated meditation on the exercises, you can comfortably pick out those that affect you the most, and scale up progressively.

When you do, start closing the cracks from there. This chapter's final exercise and those in-between are targeted at further addressing these stoppers.

YOUR MIX FOR CLOSING THE CRACKS

When you finally decide to fill up those cracks on that precious old wall, you can either get an expert fix or get it done yourself, depending on the level of the crack and its' root cause. If the root cause discovered was as a result of the defective concrete previously used, then we tag that a major crack.

To get this fixed, an expert expands the cracks intentionally to enable a thorough refill. In our lives, an expert fix comes into play when it becomes too much for you to deal with, and here in lies the need for a life coach – a need most people treat so casually.

Life coaches listen without judgments, walk you through rebuilding after those defects, and signpost you to healing when and if necessary. **Contact for an 'expert fix' will be made available by the end of this book.** However, the focus now is on addressing the minor cracks – the ones you can handle on your own through conscious efforts.

I have countlessly watched my father successfully build diverse kinds of houses from scratch to perfection, amend old houses or upgrade same to modern standards. For the amendment of cracks, if my novice self picked up a thing or two, it is that the major things needed to mend a crack is a concrete repair mix, comprising cement, sand and water.

MEND THE CRACKS

1. **Own it:** Likened to the cement which is the master element for the concrete repair mix, you need to attain a level of conscious awareness of your stoppers and own them. If you carefully treated the previous

chapter, I would love to believe you are now aware of them. It's time to own them. This does not mean accusing yourself for having them, rather accepting in the most sincerity that they are present. There really is no need lying to yourself about them or trying to shove them like they don't exist when you know they do.

2. **Address it:** Likened to the sand used to add to the density of the cement, notice that although the cement is the master element for the mix, it cannot be used alone. In our lives, owning that the stoppers exist is not enough. It is one thing to accept your stoppers as flaws, it is yet another to address them consciously. There is no success in identifying without tackling them – get rid of doubts, fear, unforgiveness, ingratitude, etc. . . In all you do, note that **"This is who I am"** can no longer work, so, be intentional about working on them.

3. **Repeat the process until mastery:** Even with the right mix of cement and sand, there is no miracle that will create a usable paste without water – the key ingredient that binds the sum together. This means that even if you own it and address it, only you can make the change long term. If water hardens the concrete through hydration, then you have to repeat your solution in consistency to build a habit, and eventually a life style – the 21/90 rule – it takes 21 days of doing a thing consistently to form a habit, and 90 days to make it your life style.

BUILD YOUR BRIDGE

Traveling from point A to B requires creating means of connectivity, and we understand that these connecting factors defer one to another, depending on the uniqueness of each person's journey. While some journeys will require building actual overhead bridges and moving on land, some might require a simple road fix, and the others might require hours of flight time, crossing seas, countries, deserts, and what have you.

In real life context, the bridge between where you are now for whatever reasons and where you want to get to needs to be connected. While you are not beating yourself up about the lack of connectivity now, you are consciously creating realistic and strategic ways to link them all up.

First things first, where are you now? Find out with the wheel of life:

THE WHEEL OF LIFE

Before you proceed to even building a bridge, it is important that you know where you are now in major aspects of your life, in relations to where you should be. Research has it that the concept of the wheel of life was originally created by Paul J. Meyer, and was designed to measure individual's current state of reality. And like a wheel, to help find out exactly how bumpy their life's ride is now.

The wheel of life is also so important to help you see the various spheres of your life, the links between them, and how to balance them out.

How to use:

- Write out 8 key spheres of your life: Feel free to use the ones listed thus - relationship and love, fun and recreation, business and career, family and friends, health and fitness, money and finances, personal growth, and physical environment.
- With a scale of 1-10, 10 being the highest (good) and 1 the lowest (bad), measure your present reality.
- Brainstorm carefully and in sincerity to get the right measures.
- For a more realistic result, measure in relations to a year from now or 5 years if that feels more realistic to you.

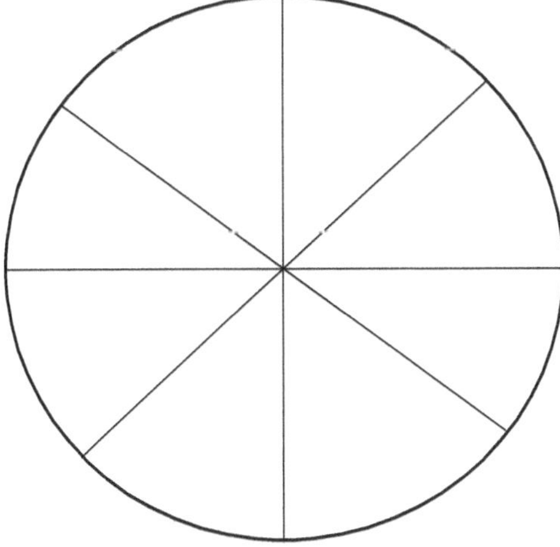

Reflection Question:

- How bumpy is my ride?
- In relations to where I want to be, where am I now?
- Are there low numbers, if yes, why?
- Were there points when the low numbers were high? If yes, what brought them low?
- Are there high numbers, if yes, why?
- Were there points when the high numbers were low? If yes, what did I do that took them up?
- How do I reconnect the bridge from where I am to where I want to be?

THE RIGHT BRIDGE THAT CONNECTS

Chances are that the moment you start building the right bridge for a sphere of your life, you unknowingly and indirectly begin to address other areas of your life. This is because rebuilding works exactly the same way destruction does, only this time in the positive. Boom and in no time, you look back and wonder how it all worked out.

When you begin to build the necessary bridges to address your career and business life, most times that bridge addresses other aspects of your life, like your finances. When your finances skyrockets reasonably and you are able to start saving and investing wisely, your living standard changes.

As your living standard changes, your physical

environment could change too, you begin to eat healthier meals, adjust your fun and recreation, and build healthy work life habits that allow you time to connect with friends and families. See how balanced out that is?

Sometimes all you need to do is ask yourself the right questions:

- Are there things I need to start doing, stop doing, pay more attention to, re-strategize, or delegate?
- Am I too rigid with my willingness to learn something that might disrupt my norm?
- Do I know what to do but scared of change?

If you are honest enough, you will see the right questions to ask, and answers to those questions. Most importantly, start taking actions today.

In all this, note that if you are building a bridge for one aspect and some other aspects don't seem to be affected positively overtime, then that's a sure indication that you need to focus on that aspect too. Always remember to focus one at a time!

THE BEAUTY OF THE STAGES OF BUILDING LIFE BRIDGES

The popular phrase "Rome wasn't built in a day" is so casually interpreted we lose an in-depth understanding of it. Life happens in stages, but sometimes we get so tempted to put a complete halt to our endeavors for the single reason it is not giving us the immediate results we want.

Reflective Illustration:

When a bridge is built to help individuals commute in their own cars from a point to the other, it is also built for those who will need to walk first, and then take the public transport means, until they finally become proud owners of their private means of commuting.

Even after you have attained the height of private commutation, would your car not lose relevance with time? If it's not to wear and tears after long usage, it will be affected by the passage of time – unavailability of car parts due to little or no production of that precise brand.

Similarly, when an airport is built to allow commuters fly with ease to various destinations, airplanes for domestic flights are separated from that for international flights in terms of standards and capacities. Even after this, each airplane still have various classes of commuters – Economy and Business classes essentially.

Rebuilding your bridge requires patience

If you have ever been at a point in your life where you are trying to overcome stagnation or reconnect your bridges and it feels like it just isn't working, then congratulations on being human.

Pause and reflect: Do you plant a seed and expect it to

germinate the next day? No? Treat yourself with more patience, less blames, staying grateful for the privilege to even rebuild, and consistently rewarding yourself for every yardstick, lest you end up belittling your endeavors, and ruining efforts. Remember this, rushing in means rushing out.

You rebuild in dimensions and with focus

One of the ways you will tire yourself is to run everywhere trying to build all the bridges at once. As discussed earlier in this chapter, you could build on one and others begin to balance out by themselves. Find out that "one" – the root of it all, and begin from there.

Pause and reflect: If your leg hurts from putting on the wrong shoe size, would you go and buy new clothes or change the shoe? Your guess is as good as mine; the focus will be on changing the shoes. Take your time to build the most "painful" aspect first – one aspect at a time, not too long or short, but also with the right amount of focus *(Chapter on finding your pace expands on this)*.

Be flexible in rebuilding

"One shoe can never fit all" is the right phrase to describe the importance of flexibility in rebuilding. You need to constantly tweak your strategy in rebuilding, and never stay stuck with a method even after you know it isn't working.

Pause and reflect: Can you imagine the amount of global dysfunctionalities and boredom that will engulf us all if one strategy could be used throughout all nations, generations, or industries in the world? In our life, this also means that using similar strategies to rebuild your career, family and relationships might be futile, and using the same strategies others used, might be counterproductive.

In rebuilding "this is who I am" can no longer work

As a result of habits and lifestyles we have formed overtime, and the discomfort of change, we are tempted to believe that the way we know is the right way to go, and the place we are, is where we belong, but, sometimes the place you are used to is not where you belong – perhaps most times.

Pause and reflect: Recall a curriculum you were taught in 1992, and ask yourself if it'd still be relevant as at 2022. Now, imagine how you will feel when you come to discover that your children are still being taught with the same curriculum... Would you tag that progression or retrogression?

No one can grow, holding on to "what it used to be"

CONNECT YOUR BRIDGE

If the gap between where you are and where you want to get to needs to be connected, take note that:

- You need to get rid of blame games – not your past errors, and not anyone else!

- You have to make the move now – not later, and not whenever you feel like it!

- You sow the right seeds according to the harvest you wish to reap in the nearest future.

- You need to close the gaps in your thoughts, to successfully close it in reality.

- You must see it before you see it, feel it before you touch it, and believe it to fast track it to reality.

- When you visualize your connection outcome, do that with a strong and stubborn desire, to win and have no thoughts on losing!

CHAPTER RECAP

10 key things to remember from this chapter

1. Life is a series of multiple connections; your spiritual life, health, finances, career/business, physical environment and relationships are intertwined.
2. Ignoring a stopper in one aspect of life can grow into 2 stoppers, then 5, until another aspect of life is affected.
3. To mend major cracks, get an expert fix (life coach). To mend minor cracks, consciously own them without accusing yourself, address them, and repeat the process until mastery.
4. The bridge between where you are and where you want to be needs to be connected to live fulfilled.
5. Your wheel of life is a useful reality check tool to help you understand where you are in relations to where you are headed.
6. Sometimes, all you need to do to build bridges is to ask the right questions, give precise answers, and take immediate actions.
7. Building, like life, happen in stages. Do not halt your endeavor because it is not bringing immediate results.
8. If you will rebuild successfully, you need patience, understanding of dimensions, focus, and flexibility in your approach.
9. Sometimes, and perhaps most times, the place you are used to is not where you belong.
10. You must see it before you see it, feel it before you touch it, and believe it to fast track it to reality.

CHAPTER EXERCISE

Complete this in your personal journal.

Now that you know your present reality through the "wheel of life", draw up a new wheel. Decide a new reality you want in 1 year, and perhaps another for 5 years and in your new wheels, draw them out. *Be realistic in your 1 year decision.*

With your understanding of connecting bridges, what aspect/sphere of your life are you experiencing the most pain, and what do you need to start doing now?

How do you think all the spheres of your life will need to be in order to connect successfully?

Your Special Treat!

After you complete this chapter, including the reflections and exercises, do something good you've always wanted to do but kept procrastinating! Applauds! Your progress gives me joy!

SECTION 2: ONE FOOT IN!

"You never know what's around the corner. It could be everything. Or it could be nothing. You keep putting one foot in front of the other, and then one day you look back and you've climbed a mountain."

— Tom Hiddleston.

IS FAILURE A THING?

"Failure is an attitude, not an outcome."

— Harvey Mackay.

The word "failure" is so loosely used!

This chapter will begin with addressing the general misconception about failure, including the pictures painted by the society, what failure is and what it isn't. But first, let us sincerely answer some questions:

Reflection Exercises:

What do you most frequently hear that failure is? _________

____

____

____

____

Do you believe in this statement: "In order to succeed, you must compulsorily fail a couple of times"? Why though? ______________________________________

____

____

____

____

Have you ever failed in any aspect of your life – maybe an exam, a task, a startup or even a relationship? If yes, what aspect and how did it make you feel? _____________________

____

____

____

How has that affected the way you now view failure

and success?____

____

____

____

____

____

MISCONCEPTIONS ABOUT FAILURE

A common societal picture painted in the mind of individuals is that failure is the only pathway to success – meaning that for anyone to attain success, they must fail. Well, if you have lived your reality this way, now is the time to rethink and overhaul that reality, as I hope you will be able to find a reason why you should, by the end of this chapter.

There are so many concepts we live by that have succeeded in making us live like we are powerless and totally unable to change the world around us. For one, as I have highlighted in chapter 2, paradigm is also seen in our definition of the concept of failure.

I grew up in an average family, somewhere in between the upper echelon and the other extreme. This subjected me to growing up in a society that had the unhealthiest concept about failure – the need for intensified struggles and the normalization of extreme hard work before you achieve success. This narrative pushed me to begin "hustling" at an age earlier than I'd have loved to, and got me into wrong hands that almost scarred me for life.

It got me feeling like I needed to struggle, suffer, and work so hard, only to receive pennies for the sweat, and finally fail before succeeding. I began to pour that equal amount of energy on others, and repelled people who I didn't see putting that much effort, as I didn't believe in the concept of seamless victories. However, even with all those struggles, I felt stagnant and dissatisfied most part of my life, even while earning.

Does this story sound familiar?

I feel so loved by Infinite Intelligence because the moment I opened myself up to learning and harnessing my potentials, I was immediately exposed to teachings that contradicted my attitude towards failure, and it wasn't long before I got connected to few people with stories of seamless victories. It then dawned on me that I had spent my years fighting battles that weren't even present, experiencing sufferings that were only happening in my mind – all imaginary.

How's it going? It has been a lot of conscious efforts completely overhauling that narrative and addressing the fear of failure already created.

THE FEAR OF FAILURE

Recall the 7 basic kinds of fear – fear of failure, ill-health, poverty, criticism, loss of love, old age and death. As discussed in the chapter on "what is stopping you", fear is a very powerful emotion, so powerful it can do exactly what faith will do for you, only this time in the negative. One of the greatest causes of failure is the fear of failure in itself. What you greatly fear has a way of showing up just as you feared it.

Here is why: Like every emotion, fear of failure comes with energy – a force that pulls whatever you are afraid of right into your life. These fears prevents some people from making an attempt, keeps some others from rising after a fall, and leave the rest suffering imaginarily.

If you tell me your life is messed up, one of the first set of questions I will ask you is what you feed into your mind – the kind of news you take in, the friends you keep, and all those basic things you do to yourself. Not to blame you but to draw out a pattern to help your understanding of how energies work.

You cannot dwell so much on negative news and expect to live a positive life. Take an instance on the greatest pandemic of our time – COVID 19 pandemic. When it started, the fear and panic was overwhelming that we unanimously created so much energy that eventually turned a few cases to multiple global cases, until it became a lock down that threw people out of a normal life, prolonged education and jobs, and forced some businesses out of operations.

Guess what happened when the fear dropped? The stories began to change and we began to live with the new normal... Has it finally fizzled out as at 2022? No, but things are beginning to go back to "business as usual".

Do you not wonder why the candidate most people detest usually wins the election? Well, energies... That is the exact effect if similar energy is placed on failure...

If you think you are beaten, you are
If you think you dare not, you don't
If you like to win, but you think you can't
It is almost certain you won't.

If you think you'll lose, you're lost
For out of the world we find.
Success begins with a fellow's will
It's all in the state of mind

If you think you are outclassed, you are
You've got to think high to rise
You've got to be sure of yourself before
You can ever win a prize

Life's battles don't always go
To the stronger or faster man
But soon or later the man who wins
Is the man WHO THINKS HE CAN

By

Walter D. Wintle

FAILURE "MIGHT BE A THING", BUT IT IS NOT COMPULSORY!

Making a conscious research on failure, 99% of articles and posts I came across spoke so concretely of failure as being "compulsory". I wasn't pleased with those and dug even deeper until I stumbled on a different blog post that opposed all other materials I had come in contact with, and it highlighted a key point **"failure does not exist"**. I bet that made you roll your eyes...

The claim from this infamous blog post was that failure only becomes a thing in our lives when we accept that it is a thing, this also means that failure only happens after you have accepted a thing as defeated. After series of logical reasoning and self questioning, I realized that the definition of failure most people have is one based off of unhealthy standards set by someone else.

Our major definitions come from the pressure of trying to use someone's lifestyle as a benchmark, the struggle to appear successful, the stubborn refusal to tweak a strategy, or the dying need to prove to someone else that we are doing just well, especially those who had told us we can't amount to anything.

If this is you, you need to stop tiring yourself with unhealthy expectations. We all have differing uniqueness, potential, Grace, and timelines. Some billionaires are made at 18, some else at 38, others at 58, and some others at 78.

Reflective Illustration:

It is common knowledge that when the front tyres of a car bust during a ride, the driver isn't expected to react by applying the brake, but to hold on to the steering as firm as possible, while directing it rightly, until it eventually comes to a halt. This is the thin line of reaction that determines if a ghastly accident will occur or will be avoided.

Reactions are everything!

I must admit that sometimes we expect the ride to be smooth, as a matter of fact, we all crave it, but that isn't the concern, the concern is our reaction to a little bump in the way. And this, you see, changes everything. Here is how it works:

- **A negative reaction** and the crave shifts, pressure is birthed, failure is defined, the course of the ride changes, another uncertain journey is born. Guess what? Another little bump in the new journey and life becomes a cycle of unfulfilled dreams and avoidable mistakes.

- **A positive reaction** and the crave stays, becomes even stronger and then adjustments are made to restructure and re-strategize the trip. In this lies your achievement of the success on the other side.

Replace those times of undue pressure with self-appraisals – progress reports, strategy developments, implementation, impact, and value addition. Success always follows.

FAILURE IS NOT WHAT YOU THINK IT IS

We are so quick to label everything that doesn't work out the way we expect them to as failure and that is the root of staying in stuck points and dissatisfaction for longer than we should. Most online dictionaries define it as "the absence of success", and if you decide to go by this definition, then I must ask you: "what is success and whose right is it to define what success should mean to you?"

Oh you didn't get that job? That does not mean you failed. Maybe you just need to upbeat your skills or expand your search. Now you are at a point of stagnation? That does not also mean you failed. Maybe you just needed this book to help you revamp on old strategies. You didn't get that admission after 4 tries? Have you thought maybe that course isn't for you?

I recall the first time I had a carryover in my undergraduate – my only carry over, I almost passed out, literally. I was so angry at myself, but my anger was short-lived when I realized my script was actually missing and never marked.

During my MBA, I had my second ever carryover. Well, I wasn't so angry this time, I knew I was so work busy to really learn my calculations, so, I probably mixed up my calculation during the quantitative analysis exam.

Sometimes, like my undergraduate carryover, it is not you; it is a careless omission by someone else. Other times, like my MBA, you are just not prepared enough for it. But like I did at both times, I never called myself a failure, not even unconsciously.

Avoid using that word so loosely... Contrary to the make belief about failure, there are a lot of things failure isn't, and they are discussed thus:

Making a mistake does not mean you failed

This might sound a little unbelievable because most times this is the picture of failure painted in our minds. Oh you made a mistake in your past relationships? I'm sorry, but you didn't fail, you only didn't know better! Now you know better, what would you do about that knowledge?

If you focus so much on your mistakes, it will be impossible to live beyond that mistake or see a brighter light. I've always believed that mistakes only teaches you what do and not to do now and in the future. And I think it is very important to let you know that there is nothing like "too late to amend a mistake". If you note your mistakes, accept it, but do something about it, whatever it is, stop wallowing in the guilt of those mistakes.

Having to wait does not mean you failed

More times than never we unhealthily expect things to work out immediately we set out on our journey, after designing what seems like the most perfect strategy. Well, the chances of that happening aren't fully guaranteed.

I have also observed that the tendency of giving up very close to victory is so high. Why this happens is a potential research worth embarking on...

Do you plant seeds today and expect them to germinate tomorrow? Obviously not! While some seeds would take few years before harvest, some others will take several years and yield fruits that will make up for the lost times – waiting for your harvest for a while doesn't mean you failed, and sometimes if you wait reasonably enough, the win will come.

I know you're forced to ask how much time is reasonable enough. My response is to keep going, wait in faith, with a positive anticipation, and an open mind to readily switch strategies, and when you least expect, you'd see your win and you'd be grateful you waited.

A shortfall in your strategy design does not mean you failed

Strategy designs are so relevant in life's journey. There are no battles won without strategies put in place, and the same applies to life in general.

However, the world in itself is beautifully complex, with ever changing needs; hence spending years designing strategies don't also mean they'd be the right ones for the commencement or throughout your journey.

You might be quick to get weary when you spent a long time building a strategy and it doesn't seem to be working out, but your ability to hold steadfast and your flexibility to adapt your strategy to fit present realities, could mark your victory.

Not getting it right the first time does not mean you failed

I know we all expect that the moment we discover our purpose and start navigating through, with much efforts, enthusiasm, and focus, our lives will immediately begin to make sense – I did too.

The day I accepted my call and began navigating my purpose, my mind opened up to all I could do. I started reactivating my childhood influences, passions, talents, gifts, skills, experiences, eureka moments and all the in-betweens, and surprisingly, what I needed to start doing now began showing up.

Suddenly, the confusion started because I couldn't exactly connect the dots. I felt knowing all these factors to purpose meant I will get it right immediately, at least that's what most motivators made me believe. Well, reality check, I didn't. However, that didn't stop me from just moving with what I had. Couple of weeks down the line, while still moving, I finally got the dot that connected everything.

The dots might not connect immediately or it might, you might not get it the first time or you might. Just never think you failed because it didn't happen the first time, and do not self sabotage your efforts because you think it is unusual to connect the first time based on other people's experience.

Being called a failure doesn't mean you failed

Everyone has an opinion about your mistakes, decisions, career path, health, children, relationship, and future, literally everything. None of which will matter if you don't allow the opinions of others shape you.

It is never what people say to you that shape you; it is 100% your acceptance of what was said as true that makes it true.

Based on people's judgment, Thomas Edison failed to refine the light bulb after 9999 attempts, but at the 10000th attempt, he got it right. The most interesting part of it all was that when asked about his failures, he said "I have not failed. I have just found 9999 ways that do not work".

This attitude is THE ULTIMATE ATTITUDE!

FACTS ABOUT FAILURE

It is not the ultimate pathway to success

Contrary to the make belief, failure is not a pathway to success because not everyone who "failed" at a thing could embrace the "shame" and try that thing again.

I know they say that a strong person falls 7 times and

rise 7 times too, but that is not an excuse for you to decide you have to fall at all. Not everyone falls, some just stagger, and some others just have long wait times, and with consistency, they'd succeed. Don't live like you expect to fail, and don't approach any aspect of your life like you think it won't work out.

Pause and reflect: If failure was truly a pathway to success, you should expect that after a divorce, the next marriage should be beautiful right? Is that always the reality? Not quite. In the same vein, would you say because there is a high rate of divorce, you have to also join the statistics?

It is an opportunity

I was not okay with my MBA carryover in quantitative analysis and I made a decision that I'd ace the course the next time I am faced with it. I totally did! Before that decision, I was among the crowd that begged for extra marks, all I needed was 3 marks to get to 40 – an E. This would have uttered my entire CGPA, and to think I was okay with that at a desperate point.

When you are desperate to cover up the failed attempt for the fear of what people will say, you miss the opportunity for a positively disruptive comeback!

It is a learning platform

A new platform to learn is guaranteed! You learn from those failed attempts, and that's what it should be. You learn how not to live, how to address a situation better, who you need to surround yourself with, the right way to go, how to shut out the wrong opinions, on and on. The problem is when you refuse to learn at all.

COUNT YOUR BLESSINGS, LEARN THE LESSONS

Every situation is a potential blessing, only if you begin to train your mind to live on this frequency, even in the midst of the storms and stagnation.

I do understand you are about asking yourself how this can be possible when you've made so many mistakes already. Understand that life is a series of conscious efforts, and so begin to consciously cast down unpleasant imaginations and take the wheel because you can!

What to do?

1. **Speak the word:** If you have gotten to this point of the book, then you must have come across the "affirmation" exercise and hopefully, written some down. However, if none of them addresses those previous mistakes, write some more that does.

    Example if you lost so much money because of wrong spending, then affirm this: "I am a smart money man/woman, and I make the right spending choices".

2. **Still your heart:** Yes, you can! That power is yours. Know that trials are potential keys to success and by stilling your heart, you are able to tune into possible solutions to overcome those problems.

3. **See the opposite of your fears, doubts and anxiety:** If you are scared you might not make it again, begin to see yourself living the life you desire. Flip the switch!

4. Change the narratives. Go about your life focusing on 1-3!

There is no defeat except that which you have accepted as such.

CHAPTER RECAP

10 key things to remember from this chapter

1. If you've ever lived your reality thinking you must fail to succeed, it is time to rethink and overhaul that reality.

2. The fear of failure is a very powerful emotion that transmits energies, and creates a force that pulls whatever you are afraid of right into your life.

3. The societal meaning of failure only becomes a thing in your life when you begin to place unhealthy expectations on yourself.

4. How you react to any bumpy road in your journey determines if you'd overcome it or stay stuck in cycles of different unending journeys.

5. Sometimes if you wait reasonably enough, your win will come – but keep going, wait in faith, with a positive anticipation, and an open mind to readily switch strategies, and when you least expect, you'd see your win and you'd be grateful you waited.

6. Failure is not what you think – having to wait, a shortfall in strategy, making a mistake, and not getting it right the first time, does not mean you failed.

7. It is never what people say to you that shape you; it is 100% your acceptance of what was said as true that makes it true.

8. Failure is a learning platform and an opportunity for a positively disruptive comeback.

9. Don't use people's experience to benchmark yours unhealthily; else you might end up self sabotaging when things work out for you smoothly.

10. Life is a series of conscious efforts, and so begins to consciously cast down unpleasant imaginations and take the wheel because you can!

CHAPTER EXERCISE

Complete this in your personal journal.

In what aspects of your life do you think you have failed? Make a list of them. For each, give a brief account of what happened.

Now, redefine failure! Repeat the activity on "count your blessings, learn the lessons" for each of them!

With the understanding you have now, how do you want to change the narratives? What would you need to do now to stop feeling like you have failed? Write it down and start now!

Your Special Treat!

After you complete this chapter, including the reflection and exercises, give yourself three rounds of applause, you could include a dance to your favorite song too, I mean, why now? Kudos! I celebrate your progress with you!

FIND YOUR PACE

"Life is a marathon, not a sprint; pace yourself accordingly."

— Amby Burfoot.

L ife was never designed in a way that gets under or overwhelming, we only complicate these things ourselves by either going too slow we lose out on opportunities, or going too fast we raise anxiety that eventually mitigate efforts. Your pace doesn't mean your speed, but just about the right amount of speed.

Every life, just like a car race is given a speed limit by which it is expected to run. The instructors that place speed limits on car races definitely understood the road construct and its' network, and possibly foresaw the dangers ahead if the racers go below the limit or above the limit. Anything lower than usual will constitute road nuisance by limiting the progression of others coming behind the racer, and any speed higher than usual will not only put the lives of others at risk, the racer's life would not escape the consequences.

Most times, we fail to understand that the outcomes of our lives, decisions, and journeys, not only affect us as individuals, but people around us, as explained in the above illustration. While a wrong pace might hinder you from grabbing or ruining opportunities, it will also directly or indirectly affect other people whose outcome is tied to those opportunities.

For instance, if you delay starting that business because of those tiny bit excuses, perhaps the fear of failing, you'd be unable to create jobs for others whose immediate survival depends on working and getting paid. Similarly, if you also pace so fast in starting those businesses for the wrong reasons, perhaps because everyone else is doing it, you might create those jobs quite all right, but would quickly scrap those jobs when the business doesn't work out.

A major characteristic of the right pace and speed is that your entire life just balances out. You have enough time to grow your career and business, while catering for your family and friends. Then you can keep your health on active check, as you also take time out to invest in your relationship and Significant other. Growing your financial strength and building wealth becomes easy, as you also manage your personal development, and inculcate the right amount of time for healthy fun and recreation.

I understand that sometimes we are tempted to do so many things at once, but if you live like this, tendencies of missing out on the most important things of life increase. So, allow yourself to grow one step at a time, and go one pace at a time.

Reflection Questions:

- When was the last time you did something because you wanted to and not because you were trying to meet up with someone else's race?
- At the time, does the pace of your journey interests you?
- When you look at the major spheres of your life, is there any you think is faster or slower than the others? Think carefully and be ready to identify them in this chapters' exercise.

LIKE MINDS AND COUNSELS, NOT COMPETITORS

It is largely discussed that one of the yardstick of an organisation's continued success is to build up sustainable competitive advantage, in relations to making their resources rare, valuable, hard to imitate, and non-substitutable, but an organisation with the key focus to only beat up competitions will fizzle out faster than it started. This is because the focus should be to maintain relevance as much as possible, not to exist only for the sake of competing.

When your plan as an organisation is to maintain relevance, your focus is centered at the right strategies, structures, processes, staffing, and all other systems that will not only work now but with consistent research and development, match up globalization.

There is no way you will put the right efforts on these, and still pay *total* attention to getting competitors out of the way. Key word: "total attention". Of course, healthy competitions could keep you on your toes; however, a total focus would be counterproductive.

I recall my days as an amateur high school athlete, my young mind would always aim at overtaking the opponents, yet focusing on my own lane, and finally to get the gold medal. You have the idea from such little age that if you face your opponents while running, you'd lose track of your own race. This teaches you that your only real contest is yourself, every other thing is secondary. I'm not so sure how we lost that as adults...

Everyone is in a unique race, hence it is totally unnecessary struggling for the position of others, benchmarking your success with that of others, or focusing on how others are running – the mistakes they are making or not making. To be less rigid, you should learn from experiences and mistakes for the sake of growth, not for the sake of criticism, and never at the expense of your own unique journey.

To find the right pace as you race, seek counsels, attract like minds, while reducing competitors to the barest.

ATTRACTING LIKE MINDS

Common knowledge maintains that no one person can solve all the problems in the world, but there are problems that continuously calls out to you and that is because it is attached to your purpose. Now, that is your problem to solve. The moment you open yourself to the possibilities of attending to those problems, you begin to attract a unique set of people – like minds.

Like minds think like you do, understands themselves enough to embark on their life's journey, and is headed where you're headed or somewhere close. This means they might not necessarily have to be directly attached to the problems you have to solve, but they might solve another similar problem that will complete the whole.

How to find them

At the point I opened up to the realization that my purpose was attached to problems connected to raising a generation of teenagers and youths who will have to become aware of their paradigm, to adjust them; behaviors, to correct them; their potentials, to explore them; purpose, to harness them; and in turn, live a life of authenticity and impact, I unknowingly started attracting people with the same goal – raise a future-focused and impact-driven generation.

It wasn't also long before I started getting speaking engagements to address teenagers and youths, assignments and projects to solidify my newly discovered focus, and every other connected tasks in between.

Note this, a 360 degree global turnaround of teenagers and youth is our ultimate focus but our journeys are broken into bits, that all makes up for the whole. Personally, I am focused on finding expressions, and have a heart for improving creativity in education and entrepreneurship. Others are focused on improving agriculture, health, entertainment, etc.

At your pace, you'd discover your authentic journey, and when you do, open up to accept them, and consciously address them. This links you to like minds and the right platforms. So, it is important that you begin to pay attention to those local, national and global problems that don't let you sleep well at night - literally.

What to do?

Pay attention to what your heart has been calling you to do. What is that particular sector whose diminish troubles you? Now is the time to identify them consciously and put pen to papers.

Start talking about it on your platforms, not as a problem analyst but as a prospecting solution provider. Learn more about these areas. Whatever may, let people know your focus is on that sector and keep building the relevance.

Finally, be on the conscious look out for events and programs with themes that are related to your subject of focus or the grander goal that you will begin to attract the moment you align, and then as you proceed, open up to begin to network with people who are doing what you are doing, or something similar.

SEEKING COUNSEL

The world is filled with people who are naturally opinionated, as a matter of fact, we all have opinions, and this means that consciously or unconsciously, we want to tell you what life should be, what you should or shouldn't do, who you ought to be like, the next step you need to take, and all other things we should have just kept to ourselves. So, when you seek, be sure they are counsels, and not opinions.

Counsels are those people with profound experiences in the race you are about to run or currently running, because they have been there and have had their own share of the challenges and victories, and although these counsels might largely take the form of mentors, they could also be those specially trained for it, or like minds with vaster experience than you.

Note that not all counsels are right counsels. If you have a passion for agriculture but go to receive counsel from someone with amazing experience in health and zero agricultural experience, you are as good as seeking opinion, which is absolutely counterproductive.

In meeting the right counsels, be sure to never stop exploring your own creativity, because no one's experience can exactly determine yours.

How to know the counsel is right?

Some years back, an ex-colleague, pseudonym Jack, made a decision to become part of a different organisation. Jack was recommended for what looked like an amazing job, so he applied, went for slated interviews and got an offer. When Jack got the call back, he was extremely excited but when we reviewed the terms of engagement, although it seemed slightly better than what he had at the time, it didn't feel like it would be worth it.

At this point, Jack and I knew he needed to seek counsel from either a career expert or an experienced mentor. He did and got a feedback to give a counter offer and let it go if his counter offer wasn't accepted. Well, he had to let that go. Not later than 3 months afterwards, he got a far better offer. How many people can be patient enough like Jack?

Initially, it looked like all hope was lost, but along came a more rewarding offer with more career prospect. The intention of a counsel is for your betterment and you will always know, like your spirit seem to bare a witness with that decision. It won't make you feel at loss, and will always reconfirm your first gut feeling. The question is: do you pay attention to your first gut feeling?

What to do?

When you begin taking actions on steps listed in attracting like minds, you also open up to meeting people with more experiences than you do. Just never be scared to ask for help, but if peradventure it is difficult for you at first like it used to be for me, then follow them closely through their platforms, see what they do, how they do it, attend their programs or any program they'd be a part of, and mirror them closely.

IDENTIFYING UNHEALTHY COMPETITION

Unlike like minds and counsels, unhealthy competitors' just flows with the tides of life, tossed here and there by winds of uncertainties and indecisions, while attaching themselves to the latest journey the closest dreamers around them have.

The commonest attributes of those competitors are their interest in everything that happens in your life – for the sake of knowledge or envy and not for contribution, their speed in taking your ideas and tweaking them to fit into theirs, a continuous claim that few years back they thought about an idea you just shared with them, and finally their constant reminder that they are ahead of you in achieving goals – their very actions make you uncomfortable.

There is a level of competition that is tagged as healthy, and these are competitions that involve being appreciated or appreciating someone doing something you'd love to do, while making efforts to achieve similar goals and attain those heights. Significantly, healthy competitions are totally void of envies that pushes one to anticipate the mistakes or failure of others.

That being said, as you look out to avoid competitors, make sure you are not the actual competitor.

LIKE MINDS, COUNSELS, COMPETITORS AND THE RIGHT PACE

Among the advantages of having like minds around you, is that attaching yourself to them paces you rightly and spurs you to forge ahead in **your own unique journey** because that journey is important to their own journey, and in a grander view, help build the blocks of solutions to a prevailing problem.

Most times, like minds play the role of accountability partners, helping with burden bearing, filling in the gaps, covering lapses, and sharing experiences to keep each other on track, and as long as you remain in, increase the confidence you need to embark on your journey and remain consistent.

On the other hand, these counsels, if and when we pay attention to them, help us manage our pace. Since they have these experiences, it is easy for them to advice on when you should begin, pause, adjust and commence again. Counsels are critical to success, so it is important to get the right ones. For me, I love going for the calm ones who are aggressively passionate, and crazy dreamers who don't believe in impossibilities. I am constantly on the lookout for them, as you should be on the lookout for those that match your aspirations, personality, and/or any of your future features.

Finally, consistent competitions is totally unhealthy for you and increases the difficulty in determining the right pace, especially because it comes with the feeling that you are running in a lane different from where you should be, your efforts are not good enough, and that every other person is getting things done except you.

In pacing right, focus on attracting like minds and counsels, and avoid anyone or thing that looks like a competition.

TIMES, SEASONS, AND THE RIGHT PACE

A reiteration – you don't plant a seed today and expect that it will germinate the next day or bear a fruit other than what you have planted today. There is a time to sow and a time to reap exactly all that you've sown, and there's nothing that will stop you from harvesting all you've sown – good or bad, except a wrong pace.

The right pace allows you the opportunity to benefit from your harvest. When you forget this concept, you might be tempted to pace so fast and constantly get burned out when things don't seem to be working out as soon as you expect.

You might do all the good in the world but miss out on your harvest because you ran faster than you should, as a result of pressures you've placed on yourself while looking for immediate results. This doesn't mean you don't expect or anticipate, it means you don't halt what you are doing now because nothing is happening immediately.

You could also think the best thing is to slow down after planting a seed, and then when it's time to harvest, you're nowhere to be found. It takes the right pace to get your harvest.

DIFFERENT PACE PER LEVEL/SEASON

If you have ever played racing attack by origindata on those earlier sets of Nokia phones, you will come to appreciate the beauty of progressively scaling up various levels as you play. Notice that although you start slow, as you go up different levels, your pace automatically increases, as well as your rewards.

However, you must also be careful not to play a level 5 like you are playing a level 2, because even though you were perfectly paced at level 2 some time ago, you can still scale up to a new perfect pace at level 5 if you are willing and ready to take up and excel at that new opportunity. Being adamant and still playing a level 5 with the same pace of a level 2 will yield no results other than repeated struggles, which will in turn lead to demotivation – feeling like you are never enough, and in extreme cases, reduce your willingness to even try again.

At the same time, you must be sure not to begin a level 2 like you are confronted with a level 5. Asides the wrong investment of energy, there is a high tendency of becoming too anxious of what level 5 will look like before it even comes. This makes it impossible to enjoy your pace.

Recall that it isn't really about the amount of speed you go, but the right amount of speed at the right time, because you could have the right speed at the wrong time, and the wrong speed at the right time.

Pay attention to this:

You might be tempted to think that your level 5 will look exactly like the game earlier mentioned, and in real life mean greater responsibilities, harder work, more struggles, extreme involvement, lesser availability, but most times, the reverse is the case, especially those times you play your cards right.

Reflective Illustration:

Unlike that game, in a real life 5-scale scenario, a level 1 might be the time your journey begins, 2 might be your learning phase, 3 might be when you start strategizing and adjusting, 4 might mean your scale up phase, and 5 might be the phase you pour yourself out to others and get things done through them. *This is however a reflection, and not generalized.*

If you are over 7 years in your career, then recall when you only just begun. . . You were probably fresh out of college, perhaps unmarried, enthusiastic about the real world, landed your first job, just enough finances to get by, with time enough to have fun and fitness, and live in a fair environment. Pace imbalance is possible at this level, and sometimes excusable, but not for so long, lest you miss your next level when it is due.

2 years into your career, you are probably now aware that your previous knowledge cannot take you so far in your career, so the need to invest in knowledge begins; you are now probably considering raising a family too, and all other things in between. Your pace will now need a new adjustment to fit your present reality if you wish to live a fulfilled life.

5 years now and everything seems to be happening all at once, you have to scale your career, continue personal development exercises, maybe start a business to keep the income steady enough to take care of your family, and live in a place comfortable enough to raise your kids, without losing focus on the bond with your family, friends, and Significant other.

You also want to eat healthy to avoid future health complications, and still save and invest for a restful future, on and on.

This is mostly the time we fall short on pacing rightly, and this hinders going to a level where we can now be comfortable enough to get things done through others, and reap the fruit of all previous efforts. If you are able to pace right here, you will not miss the next and final stage.

The final stage could be when you have become a global thought leader, living a life of impact, having mentees, staying in your dream house and choice areas, with children who are excelling in their chosen careers and making you proud, growing businesses that are employing thousands of people through others you've probably made shareholders, and Graced with time freedom.

Stagnation and dissatisfaction could happen when you refuse to revamp, and readjust your pace to fit into every new level or season.

Reflect on these:

- Using the above scenario, what is your 5 scale scenario?
- What has your pace been?

KNOW YOUR RIGHT PACE

The big question will be how to know your right pace, how to fully utilize it, and how to maintain that pace despite disturbances. Here are few pointers:

You are relevant at your pace

When was the last time you felt relevant about what you do?

Can you remember the time your inputs mattered during strategic meetings at your job, or your opinion was respected in your relationship or marriage? Can you trace that time your voice made your children gather at your feet to learn, or people were willing to hear you out as you shared health tips? Was there ever a time anyone surprisingly asked you "how did you do that!?"

If you can recall any of these examples or something similar in any sphere, then that was a right pace at a particular season.

You are energized at your pace

I have an unpopular opinion about the concept of "multitasking" – doing so many things at the same time, and working under constant pressure. While we cannot completely eradicate both from human existence because there are a lot of things struggling for our attention, we should never make it a habit.

Whenever I come across a job advert that says "ability to work under pressure or multitask", I don't bother because I don't ever believe it is a normal human behavior, or that anybody should be subjected to such torture of having to do too much at once.

Truthfully, I was once subjected to that condition of anomaly, and could feel myself constantly burnout, my mental health deteriorating, my career stagnant, with no time for friends, and my relationship at the verge of "flat line". Well, it took me breaking down to finally take a bow, and rebuild from the scratch – you read right, "the scratch". At that point, anything else was better than losing myself completely. I became energized when I succeeded in finding my pace. Do you feel energized about major spheres of your life?

You have a 360 °balance at your pace

What is the need of having all the money in the world and not have the time to train your children in the right way? Would they not grow to render your efforts futile or destroy the empire you spent years building? Is it beneficial to have an amazing career without the opportunities to go on vacations? Would it not tell on your health in the long run?

What is the point of having a great bond with your Significant other, but refuse to develop yourself? Will the love and bond not go sour when finances dry up or responsibilities increases and you cannot meet up with them?

You will know your pace is right when every major sphere of your life is balanced, and none is "crying" because you are giving others greater attention. If you feel an imbalance in any sphere with the current season/level you are in, it's time to start asking the right questions, and start adjusting accordingly.

At your right pace, you are at peace

We cannot negotiate the importance of peaceful living in attaining a fulfilled and satisfied life, and this is less disrupted when you are at your right pace.

For the simple reason your pace is the right one, you won't need to struggle to meet up deadlines, fight to fit in, battle to get your children off the list of bullies in school, stay awake all night trying to sort out relationship issues, or pursue the wrong investments because your finances suddenly nosedived... Do you feel at peace or unrest about any sphere of your life?

AS YOU PACE...

Focus on things that matter

One of the elements and confirmation of being a growing human is the presence of continued distraction - everything wants your attention, and you might get so carried away and think your attention is wanted because you are the "best person in the room".

Most times, the reverse is the case... You might be called up every time not for being knowledgeable or that your expertise is appreciated, but because everyone sees you struggle so hard to take all the Glory for team exercises or being the best parent.

I know that human need to always be seen or heard, or your impact felt, the struggle for recognition, and all that, but also know that there are consequences that follow when that is all you strive for. When this is your reality, watch out that you don't start losing touch with yourself and the real things that matters.

Learn to delegate. No one was created to do everything, not even you and not even if you can or have spent years building the skill or bagging those experiences.

Be honest about your strength

I wish to reemphasize that you should never try to be anyone else, not even someone whose life you are mirroring.

You have to be authentically you, because we are all on different assignments and no matter how you try to be someone else, it will never fit.

Even if you wish to go where the world is going, as would be discussed in the chapter on "live the moment", you still have to go in line with your strengths. For one, even with my numerical abilities, I know I have no business in any field that has to do with extreme calculations, as such when following the world, I'd take cognizance of those beyond my strength.

Also, note that because you did something for few times and it didn't turn out well doesn't mean it isn't your strength. Strengths need to be harnessed too. You cannot say because you were great at drawing at a tender age, you'd always know how to, even without building them. At times, all you'd need to do is sharpen those strengths. If you haven't already discovered your strength, take a look at these triggering questions:

- What comes easily to you?
- What do people say you're good at even when you don't seem to notice it?
- What are you passionate about?
- What can you do for unbelievable longs hours and still stay pumped up?

Never delay a prompting

Like eureka moments, prompts come as solutions to

designated problems. As I'd always maintain, we cannot all solve the problems in the world, but if you look long enough you will discover that one problem that you were purposed to solve.

If you stay too long in a problem that is your business to solve, you will pick up signals in form of ideas and solutions to them. One of the hindrances between where we are and where we should be is obedience – our response to prompts and nudges. We fail to respond immediately we should, and end up responding too late for a revelation.

These promptings are signs and could show up when there is a need to attend to behavior of your kids, or might take the form of the one key to overcoming financial struggles, or that quick solution to the problem that your organisation needs to scale up successfully.

For instance, in the course of carrying out your job responsibilities, there would be times you encounter a major mental roadblock to finding a solution to a problem the positive review of your KPI is dependent on. When you are able to impress a problem on your mind by attempting to review it critically, from a positive outlook, you get back to other less mentally strenuous things you have doing. By doing this, you unconsciously send a message to your brain to search out the best solutions, which eventually comes up as prompt of the next step to take.

A research by Mihaly Csikszentmihalyi after interviewing 96 scientists, artists and writers, realized that they worked on more than one project at a time. Switching tasks is useful, and at your own right pace, the right solution will come with the right amount of energy to be invested in carrying out that solution.

Your victory is often tied to if you obey that prompt and act immediately.

Be kind to yourself, REST

Regardless of how your life goes, you can never make progress being hard on yourself. Take a breather! Rest!

One thing I know is that you will get to the apogee of your life, lines will fall in pleasant places for you, everything will work out better than you planned it, you will finally live a life of abundance, and be able to share your story to a crowd who'd be eager to hear and learn from you. But, it will only happen if you treat yourself with kindness.

A life hack I discovered is that you'd also be able to pick yourself up again faster if you treat yourself with the same amount of kindness you treat someone who is helpless around you.

Follow your standards alone

I perceive that a lot of people get tired out trying to put unreasonable timelines and unhealthy benchmarks. By all means, aim high but make sure that "high" is not based on anyone else's standards.

Yes! Push yourself, break the barriers, enlarge your coast, expand your horizon, but let it only be because of your personal conviction of what you should be doing, and not a pressure placed on you because someone else is doing it or has instructed that you do it, and definitely not because your "role model" do it.

Personally, at the beginning of any journey, it is God – Infinite Intelligence first, counsels next, and less of opinions. It is not a good feeling when you feel the need to impress anyone, compete or push yourself beyond seen and unseen limit.

Aim ➡ Set your standards ➡ Try ➡ Do your best

Breathe ➡ Try again ➡ Win!

CHAPTER RECAP

10 key things to remember from this chapter

1. Life gets under or overwhelming when we complicate it by either going too slow we lose out on opportunities, or going too fast we raise anxiety that eventually mitigate efforts.

2. The outcomes of our lives, decisions, and journeys, not only affect us as individuals, but people around us.

3. Focus on building a network of like minds, getting the right counsels, and less on opinions and competitions.

4. You cannot solve all the problems in the world, but when you see that one problem that keeps calling out to you, begin to address them. This connects you to like minds and counsels.

5. As you follow counsels – people with an experience in your area(s) of calling, do not overlook your own unique journey.

6. Avoid people who don't actively contribute to knowledge and ideas you share with them, but instead are quick to tweak it into theirs or remind you they thought of it before you did, and act like they are constantly ahead of you.

7. If you plant a seed today, it will yield fruits in line with what was planted, the only thing that can stop you from reaping your good harvest is the wrong pace.

8. Every new level and season requires a different kind of pace. Never pace your level 5 like a level 2, and vice versa.

9. The common features of the right pace is that you are relevant, energized to carry out your responsibilities, peaceful, and have an all-round balanced life – 360°.

10. As you pace, always pay attention to the things that matters per time, never delay a prompting, be honest about the capacity of your strength, be kind to yourself enough to take breathers, and follow only your own standards, none else.

CHAPTER EXERCISE

Complete this in your personal journal.

When you look at the major spheres of your life, is there any you think is faster or slower than the others? Carefully identify and pen them down. Why do you think the pace isn't right?

With the understanding you have now, what would you need to do now to pace rightly in those spheres?

Finally, judging from the topic on life minds and counsel, what specific local, national or global problems do you think you were called to solve? What kind of people do you think you would need to attract? What would you do to attract them?

Your Special Treat!

After you complete this chapter, including the reflection and exercises, grab an ice cream, smoothie or something similar! Hurray! I join you in celebrating your progress!

LIVE THE MOMENT

"Your life requires your mindful presence in order to live it. Be here now."

— Akiroq Brost.

L et's open this chapter with something to think about!

Reflective Illustration:

In 1994, firm A introduced a product that sold so fast that as at 1997, it skyrocketed with over 400% profit from 1994. Quite an excellent jump, as you would barely see a family in literally all countries of the world without possession of this famous product.

This went on for years that as at 2007, firm A had saturated the entire market, stifled all possible competitors to manage a minute percentage of the industry's market share, while it sat on over 70% market share. In the same year, firm B; an old firm introduced a somewhat similar product that barely struggled for 5% market share.

In 6 years from 2007, there was a massive shift, as firm A's popular product declined by over 90% market share, and firm B's product's market share scaled up beyond a total and immediate comprehension of how that possibly happened.

Here is the contention, what happened to firm A? What did firm B do differently? Share your thoughts:

____

____

____

____

____

____

What could firm A had done differently to maintain their relevance? Advice:

____

____

____

____

____

When we try to analyse situations like that of firm A in the case stated above, most times we are quick to pick out the obvious and possible things that could have led to this massive decline, like bad leadership, poor staffing and training, improper structures, systems or processes, and perhaps lack of finances to scale up. Also, a critical review of firm B would suggest the exact opposite of what happened to firm A.

However, let me open your minds to a more encompassing answer to what exactly happened – **"living in the moment"**. How?

Living in the moment means living now, here, today, or at present. What we need to take cognizance of is that living in the moment can happen in four extreme sides of an equal square:

- Living now and holding on to the past.
- Living now and losing sight of tomorrow.
- Narrowly living now, with the anxiety of tomorrow.
- Living now with lessons from the past, and a focus on tomorrow.

Interestingly, in all four cases, you are living in the moment but subject to different conditions. Each of this condition further decides your fate and if you truly live or just barely exist.

Living now and holding on to the past

Except for a baby just being born into our precious world as you read this, we all have experiences and blasts from the past. These experiences might be ours, that of our caregivers or information we pick from people when they share their personal experiences on some subject matters, especially those we are yet to experience by ourselves.

Truth is we are all guilty at certain points in our lives, maybe till date, of living our present reality based on these pasts. This might not be such a terrible idea, but you see, the big question is how do you think that has affected you from actually living today?

Having something to learn from these pasts is beautiful, but never at the expense of subjecting your present life to the grips on these past. Like the chapter on stopper earlier highlighted, the past is one of the most common stoppers that leaves us suffering for things that no longer serves us, or celebrating things for so long we hinder ourselves from moving forward.

These pasts might not necessarily be in the negative, it might even be a positive experience. Oh, yes! You held an amazing program that pulled over 10000 attendees... I celebrate you, I really do, and the entire world celebrates you too. Perhaps you started out a new subsidiary and voila! It scaled up in 2 years with over $1,000,000 in profit, I am honestly so proud of you!

But here's a rare secret: "when you fulfill an obligation or complete a task successful, celebrate it, be grateful for it, but never hold on to it longer than you should, lest you dwell emotionally on it and forget to move to the next phase of your assignment".

Strike a balance, a little too much of everything is terrible to do.

Some months ago, I had a conversation with one of my coaching clients who shared largely about all she had achieved in time past - all the medals, the awards and recognitions, the promotions, and all the good stuffs, but the problem now is, all gone! When we conversed, I realized her pain wasn't because she had hit rock bottom, but largely because at a point in her life she had everything she needed and things were going her way. Sadly, dwelling so much on all she used to have hindered her from living in the fullness of her present, how much more revamping for a future.

It was important to me that she first understood her feelings were totally valid, and then the digging started. There had to be something, anything at all from the past that was an asset she could leverage on to get up again... Behold, right there, there was – her experiences. A good progress we made indeed!

Pause and reflect: Back to firm A, do you think they held on so much to their past glory they forgot to plan for the future?

Living now and losing sight of tomorrow.

Sometimes, when I see how the world is going now, I get moved to tears. It is almost like not much people care about the repercussion of behaviors, decisions, characters, and what have you. Concept "YOLO – you only live once", has been so misconstrued, most people have an excuse for living recklessly today.

I was made to understand that when someone says live now because "you only live once", they mean you have to make the best and most of the present moment, without worrying about tomorrow. Key word "worrying" – anxiety or troubles with regards to potential future problems that might not even happen. That doesn't mean you should stop dreaming, spend all your earnings in one sitting, live with reckless abandon, or harm yourself and tag it "enjoying life".

When we also get stuck at certain points, often times, we are tempted to forget that how we react to the stuck points not only determine how well we'd live today, how fast or soon we will get over the stuck point, but also how our delays will affect tomorrow.

I have come to the realization that most times people hold on to marriages and relationships that are so hurtful and abusive, partly because of what people will say, but majorly because they cannot picture a future where they are with someone new, and have to go through the whole process of reintroduction and learning anew. As a result, they rather cling to today and stubbornly stay put.

Yes, a lot of people say the grass might not always be greener on the other side, but I beg to let you know that the grass is only as green as you can see. Never stay put on uncorrected dysfunctionalities or abuses – physical, emotional, sexual, psychological, spiritual, financial, cultural or verbal.

We must all agree that learning about one's self is such a challenge, how much more having to learn about someone else. However, just as you'd not make an excuse to stop learning about your strengths and weaknesses, you can't also keep depriving yourself of the goodness that tomorrow comes with. Go all out!

Let's also not rule out the fact that you can get so engrossed with the present fortune you now possess, you fail to put things in place for tomorrow.

In terms of saving for the future, I will also always appreciate the introduction of pension into the work system; of course, those systems that allow the real idea of pension thrive. Regardless of the presence of this pension, you have some work to do to preserve your future finances even if you have abundance today.

Pause and reflect: Is there a likelihood that firm A was so relaxed and comfortable with having a whopping 70%

market share in 2007, they failed to research on the dynamics and complexity of human nature – with taste that is ever changing?

Narrowly living now with the anxiety of tomorrow

Can you remember the last time you allowed yourself really savor your meal without thinking of the need to rush up and beat the traffic, move to the next activity, or worry about the next meal to cook?

I know how it gets when you have to hunt for the next better paying job, plan to have a wedding that becomes the newest sensation among your ex college mates, rush to get the new car because everyone on social media looks richer than you, or bombard yourself with drugs because you were told an ailment is hereditary, and if it happened to the generations before you, it will happen to you...

But... Pause! Breathe! I mean it – DO IT... *deep breaths*

The advice isn't to make me your alibi in living recklessly or at levity, but to remind you that there's never any pleasure derived from living on edge, only anxiety and life with millions of complaints, leading to non-fulfillment and prolonged suffering.

Oh, you were raised by extremely disciplined parents, or made a mistake while you were younger, and you automatically think the best way to "save" your children from your own mistakes is to raise them like slaves – lock them at home and refuse them socialization? Do you consider the harm that will do to their esteem in future?

When your mind is too busy worrying about tomorrow, you might never really live enough for the right solutions to come.

Even if you are struggling to make ends meet today, would that be reason enough to fail to enjoy the life you now have? Here is a secret I learnt during a leadership training: Most times, the solution to your inability to achieve anything is to go back to "a place of wait", not going everywhere seeking solutions that might never come.

Feeling like you don't fit in might become a thing too, but that doesn't mean you should live any less. You are important, and before you attract anyone that sees that in you, you must first see that in you, and rise above the noise of those not seeing it in you. There's no point living too careful today when there's a whole lot you can live for.

Pause and reflect: Why do you think firm A didn't make an early adjustment when they noticed their decline? Do you think they got scared of their competitor's products and anxious they might never meet up?

Living now with lessons from the past, and a focus on tomorrow

When my maternal grandmother joined the Angels on

the 6th of December 2019, it was one of the most shattering moments for me. Anyone would say she lived long because she was about 86 at the time, but for me, I wanted more of her, and had more to give her, I mean, we discussed about it as often as I was with her.

You know, it's not as though we don't know they'd be gone, we just hope and pray they stay longer...

Just like my Mum, she taught us values through folklores – "iho" in my native language" – the best way she knew how to. We certainly had our conflicting views on some subject matters because of generational dynamism, but we always stroke a balance. She was called "Office" by everyone around her because she was everyone's go-to person when they were stuck at any point in their lives.

Her demise attempted to halt my life, because I made promises to her that I never fulfilled. The thought of having failed her crippled my mind from dreaming for a while. I curled back, existed, and held on to the past promises and memories, throwing the future away. You'd understand the effect if you've ever been in similar boat.

It took me quite a while to realize that I could also reflect on and get joy from the past, re-live the memories today with those that I love, and dream yet again. What was most important to me was my ability to consciously pick the lessons her demise taught me:

- The past will only matter if you can make good use of them.

- Now is the time to decide what to be remembered for.
- Tomorrow is possible, but that depends on you, no one else.

Does the above experience sound familiar? It is time to pick your lessons from yesterday, build on today, with a focus on tomorrow.

Never forget where you are coming from, but never lose sight of what is ahead of you.

If you ever feel like your pasts are so important in living today, then embrace them with an understanding that they are lessons for things to do, not to do, correct or realign, and not as stumbling block or basis for judging today or what tomorrow will be.

The suffering of your parents or people close to you does not and should not automatically become your reality, and that decision is yours to make. Similarly, your parents' dynasty should not be an excuse to live without planning for tomorrow.

It doesn't matter where you are coming from, you can make a decision - good or bad - that can change the entire trajectory of your life, even to the next generations.

YESTERDAY FOR TODAY, TODAY FOR TOMORROW

Everything about our present reality is a function of things we did or didn't do yesterday – habits, procrastination, friendships, relationships, decisions, thoughts – what was treated as important that shouldn't have, and what was handled at levity, that wasn't supposed to be.

How are you living?

When you do take the time to answer this question, and have a sincere reality check, you will come to realize that there are present circumstances that could have been avoided if you took a different turn yesterday, there are excuses made yesterday that is being paid for today, there are blessings being received now that wouldn't have been possible if you didn't take that bold step yesterday.

Truth is that there is mostly nothing happening today that cannot be traced back to that one right or wrong move – decisions, choices, excuses, lies, procrastination, efforts, and kind words from yester years, save those minute unexplainable life mysteries.

An understanding of this is never for a life of regret but for knowledge, and with this knowledge, would you not plan for a greater tomorrow? Start when you need to, halt if you have to, design a different strategy, take a new turn if it is required, and avoid drooling over what isn't working and glory over the fact that you have the opportunity to make those adjustments now.

Today is a seed

When anyone tells me they cannot go back to school because they have come of age, I am forced to ask their present age, the years it will take to complete the education, and how old they'd be by then.

Pause and reflect: Assuming you are 45 years today and would love to study law that takes 6 years, but feel you are too old to join young lads in class now. My question to you is this "in 6 years from now, how old will you be whether you study law or not?"... It is an obvious answer.

This means that it doesn't matter whether you go for your dream of becoming a lawyer or not, your age is a constant – doesn't increase or decrease based on your decision, but guess what happens years from now if you don't chase that dream? – Regrets, anger, non-fulfillment, and their relations. Why not plant the seeds now and reap it tomorrow?

A life well spent is a function of a series of conscious efforts

Whether you choose to consciously plant the seeds of good friendships, investments, education, great family, and healthy meals by yourself, or leave it open to chance to plant whatever seeds are influenced by reason of your excuses, levity, procrastination, and indecision, it will germinate in the nearest future and become a fruit from what was planted – either what you bargained for or not.

I wish to reiterate importantly, that you do not plant a seed in one sphere of your life and leave other spheres. Example, you cannot be growing your career/business or finances, and neglect the place of planting seeds in good health or your family. If as a parent, you refuse to pay attention to the needs of your children at an early stage, the society has an "amazing" way of helping you pay attention to them and feed them all manner of helpless garbage.

There are countless cases of avoidable experiences and dysfunctionalities that scar a lot of adults that would never have happened; if parents paid attention when they were children... it remains a continuous cycle if the right seeds are not consciously planted.

Little can no longer be enough

It is easy to misrepresent the concept of living the moment as being comfortable at a position you are in, but that is definitely not the case.

As a result of the nature of what I do – helping people become better versions of themselves, and seeing them through on implementation of goals to attain that height, I try to dedicate some fair amount of time on relevant social media pages. On one of such days, I saw a post that triggered me and I'd share it in an abbreviated version, thus:

"Allow people to live how they like, not everyone can be ambitious, some are just comfortable with where they are – the little they are and have and that is okay too".

I beg to debunk the above statement with a million reasons – of course not literally, because I'm not about writing a million whys. While everyone cannot be equally ambitious and chasing after the big goals like the 1% of the 1% do, recall our illustration of the beauty of a tree in the chapter on "what is stopping you", the truth remains – you were never created as a finality, so quit playing small.

Life could give anyone a little cup of coffee but it demands a higher level of dreaming, active chasing, commitment, and persistence, from anyone it decides to make the brewer.

When you approach life, approach it from a place of understanding that you are so powerful and I really wish I can see you face to face and explain this, I wish I can make you understand that nothing you are going through or have today can be compared to all you're capable of getting, if and only if you refuse to embrace littleness!

CHASE AFTER THE WORLD

Globalization and generational dynamism are perhaps the most obvious reasons for the difference in expectations, and continuous need for improvements in functionalities and strategies to match up the changing times. This means that having known it yesterday does not necessarily give importance or relevance to it today. In living the moment:

Go where the world is going to

Living satisfied and in the moment requires staying relevant, and relevance with the evolving world would mean going where the world is going, but being mindful that you don't lose yourself in the course of this.

It is necessary that while you go where the world is going, you channel your strength in the right direction. I recognize the importance of information technology in our present day and years to come, and thankfully, there are a whole lot of options available for you to choose from, so choose what fits. If it is not in alignment with your strength, don't do it because everyone else is doing it. There are tons other things that will forever be relevant, pay more attention to what matches your capability, to avoid struggling unnecessarily.

If you own a business, going where the world is going might mean moving past just traditional marketing to digital marketing, improving an existing product or introducing a new service line, focusing on propagating work life balance, whatever it takes to help you structure to fit the world.

During one of my speaking engagement, a cosmetologist was curious about the place of compromising standards while going where the world is supposedly going. She had observed that majority of her peers in the bid to beat the increased global demands and make excessive profits, have switched from making purely organic products to including chemicals.

In response to this, I was very particular about the need to maintain integrity, and draw a line in the sand as to standards she will never compromise, because righteous gains are long term profitable, and give a sense of satisfaction.

Furthermore, the need to improve her strategies to reach people who would rather have an organic product that will keep their skin healthy and not pose a threat to their internal organs in the nearest future, which is the harm continuous use of chemicals, will create.

Remain Teachable

You learnt it at the University the previous year? Oh great, this year is different, so, learn how it is done this year.

Your parents raised you and defined family in a certain way that helped you grow up disciplined and with the right morals? That's perfect, but never a yardstick to raise your family the exact same way – remember generational dynamism? A value imbibed in you in a particular way, might need to be tweaked to make any impact in the lives of the coming generations.

During the years I just begun my career, and perhaps till date, the ability to learn, unlearn and relearn is one of the requirements of getting a great job. This also applies to life in general, as one needs to be open to being teachable. However, pay attention to learning from like minds, counsels and not competitors.

What to do:

Review the various spheres of your life and look at the world, where does it look like the world is going to?

LIFE IS FIRST A GAME, BEFORE IT IS STRATEGIC

The Game

You expected to hear the game life is? Let's start with literal games.

As a dominant choleric, I might often time give off the vibe of an overly serious person, but know this day that I play a lot, a whole lot. I enjoy healthy games a whole lot some friends call me a social sanguine. Simple advice: Stop making excuses with temperaments or zodiac signs.

Was I always that playful? No, especially because I didn't grow up as a very jovial kid but did I change that? Yes, because it was no longer serving me and it got so unhealthy to be serious at all points. I discovered that one of the secrets to a happy life is knowing when to play - literally.

Late in 2020, I was stuck and didn't know what to do, then I got a game card, yes, you read right. The covid-19 lock down had just narrowly been lifted and with the total disruption it caused, I wasn't having anything easy, like most people. On one of those days, I walked into a popular eatery in my city of residence – Lagos, Nigeria, to eat and think, but then a section in the eatery had a game centre! I decided to become a child for some minutes and that gave me answers I wouldn't have thought out if I stayed too uptight. Till date, when I feel worn out or stuck on getting the right ideas, I play some games!

If you will win at life, you need to see it as a game too

The exact enthusiasm you use in playing games should be the same you use when approaching life. Games come with challenges too but enjoyable challenges, as you strive to win a car race, beat previous high scores, build a better castle, or cook meals faster to feed waiting customers.

It is difficult to see someone who gives up on winning games, we only get some rest and rethink a new way to play the difficult level, and then come back to the challenges over and over again until we record a win. Imagine if you treat life like this?

The Strategy

Life is in phases, learn to adapt to each phase. If it requires you adjusting what used to be the norm for you, adjust accordingly. If your present phase is pleasant, adaptation could also mean learning new things or investing more. We all don't know what the next phase will be, but that is not an excuse not to strategize for it.

Do you remember candy crush? Every new level looks more complicated than the previous, but the way you rethink different new strategies to overcome new levels is the exact way you strategize for your next level in real life context.

As you live the moment, play as often as you can and revamp your strategies in all spheres of your life, not only to beat the new challenges that will unavoidably come, but to stay relevant as you progress.

CHAPTER RECAP

10 key things to remember from this chapter

1. You can live now and hold on to the past, live now and lose sight of tomorrow, narrowly live now with the anxiety of tomorrow, or live now with lessons from the past, and a focus on tomorrow.

2. Having something to learn from your past is great but never at the expense of subjecting your present to the grips of the past.

3. When you fulfill an obligation or complete a task successfully, celebrate it and be grateful for it, but never for too long so you don't get so emotional about it, you forget to move to the next level of your assignment.

4. YOLO really means making the best and most of today, without worrying about or losing sight of tomorrow.

5. The grass on the other side is only as green as you can see.

6. When your mind is too busy worrying about tomorrow, you may not live enough for the right solutions to come.

7. Everything about our present reality is a function of things we did or didn't do, so, live right, plant the right seeds, and never accept littleness.

8. In living the moment, chase the world, do what is within your capability, and remaining teachable.

9. Give yourself sometime to unwind and literally play games too, great ideas are birthed here.

10. If you will win at life, you need to see life as a game, and play each level like you'd play an actual game.

CHAPTER EXERCISE

Complete this in your personal journal.

Close your eyes, take your mind back to 5 years ago from today (the day you read this book). Now, think of 5 things you told yourself you were going to achieve, write them out, whether you were able to achieve them or not.

For those you couldn't achieve, can you trace the reasons why? Was it money, what people said, lack of the time to? Whatever reasons you can think of, write down. Never for regrets, but for knowledge. Now ask yourself, do I still want them? With the knowledge you now have, what would you need to do differently?

Next, close your eyes and envision 5 years from today, what 5 things would you love to achieve? You can include the things from 5 years ago and those from your 100 (refer to chapter one's exercise). YOU CAN DO THIS!

Your Special Treat!

After you complete this chapter, including the reflection and exercises, find out a game centre and go play some gram, with your mind open! Bravo! I celebrate your progress with you!

SECTION 3: NOW WHAT?

"Infuse your life with action. Don't wait for it to happen. Make your own future. Make your own hope. Make your own love. And whatever your beliefs, honor your creator, not by passively waiting for grace to come down from upon high, but by doing what you can to make grace happen... yourself, right now, right down here on Earth."

— Bradley Whitford.

POUR IN, POUR OUT

"Happiness is a perfume you cannot pour on others without getting a few drops on yourself."

— Ralph Waldo Emerson.

No matter how much we try to paint it, you cannot give what you do not have, not love, friendship, forgiveness, happiness, and definitely not a life of abundance or anything else. Do you sometimes wonder why a particular thing is difficult for you to do to/for others? Then I'd like you to ask yourself "do I do this to/for myself?" You might need to start from here.

During one of my random conversation about love with a new acquaintance, her arguments were firm about never giving out so much love to anyone in a relationship, because she has come to a conclusion that nothing good comes from love or relationships. That mindset broke my heart! Remember the earlier chapter on the magic of the mindset? Yes, we don't rule out the roles our experiences play in the decisions we make, neither do we belittle its' effects, but would that be a worthy excuse to stay in an unfavorable position forever? Would it be worth it?

Let me first express that if you find yourself in a repetitive awkward reality – a cycle of wrong relationships, continuous bad grades in a particular subject, toxic friendships, prolonged suffering, or the inability to succeed in certain things, then be mindful of what you've said about that subject matter in time past.

Whether you think you can or cannot, you are absolutely right!

Well, here was my counter view – with an understanding that it is impossible to pour out what you don't pour into yourself, I asked her, "do you love yourself?", then got the swiftest defensive response from her "what sort of question is that? I love myself so much". Then I asked "how much and how do you know you do?", and that was followed by a deafening silence before I continued... "If you love yourself so much, you will give yourself the privilege to love"

...the privilege to love others too.

My concern with having a mindset similar to what she had before we conversed is that it opens you up to a web of repeated negativity. There's no way to dismantle a 4-legged table carefully crafted with the most quality wood, by calling a carpenter to build another leg for it. In the same vein, dismantling the power or grip of your negative experiences on you isn't finding more excuses to support it; it is uncovering more counter reasons against it.

Do not also make the mistake of limiting "love" to relationships or a Significant other, friendship, or family. It encompasses your health, finances, and every other sphere of your life. If you love yourself, you will pour so much in that there is an obvious overflow, enough to even pour out to someone else.

So, I ask you my dear reader, how much do you love yourself and how do you know you do?

How much to you love yourself enough to refuse to stay stuck at a point for so long? How much do you love yourself enough to watch your diet habits? How much do you love yourself enough to walk out of unhealthy situations? How much do you love yourself enough to upbeat your skills for a career leap? How much do you love yourself enough to forgive your past experiences? How...much...? How much are you willing to pour into yourself?

You see, this influences if you ever find answers to your questions, if that peace, happiness, balance, abundance, and satisfaction ever truly happens to you. Crucially, if you are able to pass it on to someone else, this, to me, is an ultimate win for humanity.

POUR IN

Someone once told me to my face that I wasn't indispensible, and no human being is. While a lot of people will over analyse or pick an offence in that, especially after they must have giving their best and put all possible efforts, I decided to build so much relevance no one would ever be able to say that to me. So, I started pouring in and promised myself never to stop, and I haven't till date. . . Here are few pointers:

Learning

You cannot say you are pouring into yourself and

elude the significance of learning. Learning is a continuum. Learn about yourself again – strengths and weaknesses - do whatever it takes to belittle your weakness and solidify your strengths, discover your personality and how it is and can affect your behavior, take that new course, sign up for the new program, read positive and challenging books... keep pouring in new knowledge.

When you have a pain point, make it a "learn" point

The above word of wisdom was adopted during a teaching on greatness by my Lead Pastor, Yemi Davids and has become a principle I live by. When I discover a pain, I address it by learning from people who surmounted similar situation.

If an area is of concern to you, make that area a point of learning. For instance, if your finances are so bad for so long, learn from people who overcame it and books that addresses it; If you in a constant struggle with your love life, pay attention to the right relationship counsels and books too; If it is parenting that is the pain point, then attend classes that tackles it, on and on.

Positive self-talk

What are the first words you say to yourself when you wake up? What do you say to yourself when things don't seem to be working as you'd have loved it to? What do you say when someone speaks negativity into you? Do you accept it as true, allowing yourself discover more evidences that encourages that claim, or do you refute it, uncovering more evidences to knock down its' momentum?

You are first the things you say to yourself before you are what anyone else says

Say right after me: I am a star born to illuminate and dominate. I achieve everything I set my mind to. Wealth is my inheritance and I am living in an abundance of it. I succeed at things my parents or ancestors failed at. My health is perfect without struggles.

Now, it's your turn, say something positive about that situation now!

Positive self talk is not day dreaming, it does not mean problems don't exist in particular areas of concern, it means those problems don't define you. With this, you begin to open up yourself to answers and solutions that will address these problems.

Nothing short of the right company

There is a common saying: "show me your friends and I will tell you who you are". The caliber of people you keep around you or let into your space determines if you'd ever emerge and become all you were called to be, or just wander on the face of the earth. . . Read it again.

The future is too bright to surround yourself with the

wrong circle. Pour into yourself the right company of friends, like minds, and accountability partners. You deserve to have the right circle around you, a circle that motivates you, picks you up, see you through on tasks, and all the in-betweens.

10 friends cannot play for 10 years

Always remember that not everyone was designed to be in your life forever. There are friends for different seasons in your life, and there are those for every season. Sometimes you see the sign a friendship season has ended, sometimes you might not, and other times you plainly ignore them. You need to stop tiring yourself trying to "make it work" all the time!

While you don't give up on friends because you have minor rancor here and there, you don't hold on when you know it's unhealthy, toxic and competitive. If you'd be candid with yourself, you'd agree with me that most times you always know when you should draw the line, but do you?

Allow yourself to explore your uniqueness

This is coming here again, just in case you have gotten carried away with the fact that you are a very unique person, and as such, should be open to giving yourself the go ahead to explore that uniqueness. Be unapologetically you, no one else.

On days I feel unsure; I walk to the mirror and admire myself. I am a firm believer that the Creator is such a creative, I mean, if you just take a quick peep outside your window during the day, you'd see tens and hundreds of different people - body feature, walking habits, and mannerism. Isn't that enough to know no one can be you?

If you find out you are good at a thing, try to be exceptionally good at it.

For one, I decided to write this book because someone once told me I was good with words, and even though I had written couple of blog posts, learnt copywriting, been a content developer at an IT firm, created my own unique social media contents, I might never have brought myself to doing this. Most times, we might not discover these things ourselves, so be open for someone telling you what they have observed you do better than anyone else.

Open up to be helped

Pouring in doesn't always mean it is from you to you, it could also be from someone else to you.

You cannot do it all, allow room for others to

I didn't grow up receiving external helps, it was just my parents and siblings, and by extension, I learnt to do things for myself, without asking anyone for help. Since it wasn't something I was used to, it didn't make sense to me why I needed to cry for help when I'm battling with my mental health, when my finances are low, or when I am lost and confused. Well, I suffered the repercussion time and time again, until I decided, never again!

Does this sound familiar? I know you want to feel independent, but please stop struggling trying to do it all by yourself. If you are stuck, speak up, if you are broke, open up, and if life stops making sense to you, talk about it. It is very okay to be vulnerable, but be sincere.

We can't rule out the fact that some people might just want to hear your problems for the sake of hearing or mocking, but don't let that stop you. If you are worried your struggles will be the next topic of discussion, get expert help from a professional outside your circle, with no affiliations, and an oath of confidentiality. Let me state this here, be very mindful that you don't put all your hopes on being helped by others, that you get tempted to feel entitled. Strike a balance.

Take care of yourself

I need you to understand the true concept of taking care of yourself, it is not about going out to prove a point or lavishing yourself with expensive stuffs you cannot afford to please people who obviously don't care, it is the little things that count.

It could be dancing to your favorite genre, rearrange your home space, clearing your environment, gifting yourself with something affordable but valuable, eating healthy meals, taking guided meditation sessions, doing something you love, writing a love letter to yourself, ignoring your inner critic, overpowering your negative thoughts, or even checking in on yourself to know how you are at certain points.

Lastly, never be scared to put you first too, that is not selfishness, until it is done in the extreme where no one else matters but you.

Spend quality time with you

This is perhaps the most compulsory thing to add to your life's hack. We all need holidays outside of people – not those once in a year vacation we subject ourselves to.

Don't wait for the big breaks

For me, I made it a once in two weeks habit to just be by myself, away from work, phones, television, social media, or any distraction, just by myself, digging inwards, appreciating my journey – no complaints at all, allowing myself dream again, ideate and plan. For every time, I could feel myself recouping lost energies and expanding for fuller expressions.

It might be few hours in a day for you, or an entire day in a week, just make sure you are doing anything but complaining or fighting yourself for mistakes or the negative stuffs.

Reflective Illustration:

The next time you are able to walk into the bathroom, go with a little bucket if you don't already have one in. Then, turn on your tap and allow water rush in and when you are sure it is filled up, turn off the tap and observe these two things:

1. The water will remain turbulent, spiral and deep even after you have poured enough water, and it will go this way for a while before it settles.
2. When it eventually settles, you will realize that because the water came down rushing, the bucket never actually gets filled up. It was just a make belief.

How does this translate to our present living? As you pour in, take cognizance of the following:

- No principle will immediately present an obvious result, not until you pause and pour the right proportion – no hurries.
- You will only get what you are ready for, lest your hurriedly lose what you received without preparation.
- If you choose to rush the success process, the turbulence might never stop.
- If it is all you do, learn to be patient as you pour in.

AFTER POURING IN...

Value is added and paid for

People don't buy your product or services because they like you, maybe the first time, but a repeat purchase only happens when they perceive value addition. Do you make a repeat purchase if the previous item don't meet up to your expectation or add value to you? When you pour inwards, you create room for you to learn and build self value enough to be valuable to others, and when people perceive that you add value to them, they are willing to do what it takes to win you over.

Worth is rebuilt

As a result of the activities that you will be doing as you pour inwards, like the positive self talk, adjusting your circle, exploring your uniqueness, learning again, and all other activities, you begin to perceive your won worth, and sometimes, unconsciously repel everything and everyone that tries to make you feel less of who you are and can be.

Definitely not given to pride, lest you fall, but given to an understanding of all that you are capable, and an acceptance of these capabilities.

You are filled enough to pour out

There is a place for everyone to play their individual role and become a blessing to humanity, and because a life of purpose and meaning is subject to this, you get to finally attain a life of extreme satisfaction when you pour out. As you pour in, there's something to pour out.

POUR OUT

If you look around you, and the only person's life you've touched is yours, then what are you doing to yourself? The common human mind is driven by "self" – the need to pour in all the time, but pause, for a second and think of others.

One of the greatest sources of satisfaction you'd derive is from pouring out to others. We might be forced to think it is really all about financial giving, but it goes beyond that to pouring out your time, lending a shoulder, being a healing hand or a non-judgmental listening ear, signposting to the right channel, teaching people how to "fish" rather than giving them fishes all the time, connecting someone to a helper, and so on. Here are major pour out avenues:

Purpose vs. passion

Purpose is perhaps the greatest platform to pour out. The discussion on purpose is so broad and beyond few lines of texts that would be written here, but this should serve as a little but significant pointer.

One day during our support group gathering for "just an escape", we had a purpose walk and invited a well-trained purpose life coach to join me in buttressing on the consequence of living a life of purpose, to our tribe members. After so much insightful discussions, the most striking phrase for that day was "your passion is for you; your purpose is for others". Read it again...

I could guess that you have heard on several occasions that your passion might not create wealth, well, your purpose can and will, if you discover it and continuously harness it. Don't ever mistake the both; your passion is only a little part of the whole that makes up your purpose.

Reflective Illustration

I'd take the time to describe purpose in a pretty understandable term:

The Creator sees something missing on planet earth that desperately needs to be filled up, and then hands it to the next creation, *YOU*, and sends you to the earth to fill up that void. Got it? Your purpose/core reason of creation is that part of you that once found will be an avenue for you to contribute your own quota to the betterment of humanity.

In an abridged version, here are 5 key places to look to, when you begin your journey to a life of purpose:

- **Upward to your Creator:** It is noteworthy to know that only the designer of a "thing" knows fully well all what that "thing" is capable of. You can't rule out the place of God in discovering why you were sent to earth at the precise year, month, day, hour, minute and second.

- **Backwards to your childhood wonders/dreams and talents:** What did you say you'd be when you grow up?

What were you good at, whether harnessed or never harnessed?

- **Inward for your passion/interest, gifts, skills, personality, and qualities that describe you:** What can you do for free? What do you spend hours doing and never get tired of? What do people say you're good at but you sometimes never see it? Are you an introvert or extrovert, thinker or feeler? What qualities describe you? What are those values you can't compromise?

- **Outward to the categories of people you most frequently attract and your pain points:** Find out if they are children, teenagers, youths, men, or women; those who are stuck, experiencing relationship issues, battling anger, impaired, on and on. What about the world gets you hyped the most and angry when it's not working?

- **Forward to the future:** What does it look like you'd love to spend the rest of your life doing? What are the most frequent ideas for the future that keeps popping up as eureka moments?

Although not extensive, the above is a good start point.

One of the major reasons why a lot of people don't live up to purpose is because a lot of focus is placed on the physical environments and other external factors, and less on the internal factors that matter the most. While some others that eventually connect the "purpose dots" are quick to give that up, for minor turbulences.

Moving forward, if you have connected the purpose dot, excellent, but if you haven't, while you still try to connect the dots that points you to purpose, as is largely advised, go about your day to day activities exploring other "pour out" avenues.

Reach out

When you go through a pain point in your life, most times, you go through it so that when you overcome that phase, you can reach out to others going through the exact phase and help them overcome it. Rare occasions, you might begin to overpower those pain points the moment you start pouring out, because you'd need to learn to teach others about them.

You might go through stuck point so you can help anyone who experiences it when you finally overcome it. You could be going through health challenges, so that when you overcome it, you can guide someone else on how to. It could be a financial breakdown after having so much, so you can help teach people financial education. The bad times might be a blessing after all... as long as you refuse to stay there for too long.

One more thing, get rid of that mindset that everyone else should struggle to get a thing, because you struggled to get it too. If we live by that, humanity will be doomed for sure. Every new generation ought to be an improvement from the old, so, make it easy for the next person.

Be someone's mirror

Based on uncommon opinion, the reason why most people don't identify with motivational speakers is that most share pain points, exaggerate their experiences, and end up telling you "you can do it", but rarely tells you the true story about how they did it, to serve as a guide for you.

Be a person's reason not to give up, not their point of pressure

Pouring out is not about just sharing your experiences to keep people inspired and motivated, or telling them how you grew a business from 0 to $1,000,000 profits, it is about being honest in telling them about the challenges you encountered, the steps you took, the highs and lows, and the in-betweens. Never hold back knowledge!

Give to someone who can't give you back and expect nothing in return

I've sat with really amazing people who say they are only interested in giving to their family members. Truth is, they always have justifiable reasons why, but best believe that giving is beyond fulfilling all righteousness, satisfying your conscience, or being a point of rescue for your circle of family and friends.

A mindset to correct today is that you don't give because you have in abundance, you do because you were designed to be a channel of blessings, so it really isn't about what you give, it is about the intent of giving.

Importantly, except sharing is to motivate others to imitate your kind gesture and begin to give like you, give in silence.

Love, a healing energy

If the world had enough love and everyone gave it freely without holding back, the energy it will create will be so enormous it will heal poverty, anarchy, biases, unemployment, greed, corruption, wars, and every trace of negative vices, simply because everyone will learn the importance of treating everyone else like they truly matter, because we all do, equally.

Even if you decide to be anything in the world, make sure a channel of love is a part of it.

Love will make you put yourself in the shoes of others, guard your tongue while speaking lest you break their spirit, forgive wrongs done to you without planning to payback, cease to backbite on people, teach you to address issues rather than harbor them, on and on.

When you still don't know what to do, love up on humanity... Pour out so much love you begin to heal "you". .

.

CHAPTER RECAP

10 key things to remember from this chapter

1. It is impossible to give what you don't first have. So, if you'd be able to give out love, forgiveness, abundance, all positive vices, you must first give it to yourself.
2. Whether you think you can or cannot, you are absolutely right.
3. Pour into yourself so much your relevance is build overtime and dispensable can no longer describe you.
4. Pouring into yourself entails learning, positive self-talk, getting the right company, exploring your uniqueness, opening up to being helped, taking care of, and spending quality time with yourself.
5. As you pour in, no principle will immediately present obvious results, not until you can pause and pour the right proportion, in patience.
6. After pouring in, you add value to yourself, rebuild your worth, and get filled enough to be able to pour out.
7. Purpose is the greatest pour out platform, and unlike passion, your purpose is designed to impact on others.
8. Some keys to discovering your purpose is looking upward, backward, inward, outward, and forward.
9. Reach out to people, become someone's mirror, give to someone who can't give you back, and expect nothing in return.
10. Love is the greatest healing energy. With love, the world becomes better simply because it teaches us to treat each other like we all matter equally.

CHAPTER EXERCISE

Complete this in your personal journal.

What are those things you have discovered are difficult for you to do for other people? Are you pouring enough of that into yourself? If it doesn't seem so, where do you need to begin from?

Decide your pour in pointers based on what was listed out for you, and how you will inculcate it into your routine. Write them down; including when you will begin... the earlier you take an action, the easier it is to beat the temptation of procrastination.

Finally, here's an important exercise for you:

Who would you pour out to after this task? What would you do differently?

Your Special Treat!

After you complete this chapter, including the reflection and exercises, especially the pour out exercise, get yourself your favorite "any edible" – snack or meal or drink! You did excellently well! I am grateful you are a blessing to humanity, posterity will forever celebrate you!

MILESTONES ARE GOLDEN

"Remember to celebrate milestones as you prepare for the road ahead"

— Nelson Mandela.

The worst thing you would do to your journey is to ignore your milestones or act as though they are nothing serious. It is serious that you decided to embark on this journey, very serious you started taking actions after setting those goals, and even more serious that you refused to back down regardless of the forces that attempted to work against you.

Milestones are golden and cannot be overlooked, especially because not everyone who sets out on a journey ever smash the next goal, let alone arrive at their destination. Looking to get to a destination involves setting goals, and milestones are associated with reaching these goals to determine if you can now proceed to a new goal, revamp your strategy for the previous goal, or halt completely.

This chapter further buttresses on the significance of defining your desires or the destination for each sphere of your life, and setting goals to get to your desired destination. With the end in mind, it is easier to define checkpoints to make it easier for you to know when you have achieved a milestone in your journey, and the next height to attain, to get you much closer to your desired destination.

Reflective Illustration:

How often do you see schools that allow students conclude various classes or levels without breaking it into terms and semesters? I haven't, have you? These terms and semesters are checkpoints to measure progress to a milestone, and although examinations per term or semester aren't actual tests of knowledge, they determine the preparedness of a student for the next level.

Where I come from, secondary schools, also known as high schools in some other part of the world, run for 6 years long – 6 classes, and have 3 terms per class; Bachelor's degree in universities run for 4 to 6 years, having 4 to 6 levels, depending on your choice course, with 2 semesters per level.

While the end point or destination in the illustration above is to graduate from secondary school with an outstanding WAEC result or bag your Bachelor's degree, your milestones are the classes and levels you will need to successfully pass to get to that destination. Your checkpoints on the other hand are those terms and semesters that will be used to determine your fit for each new milestone.

With this structure in mind, you know that you will need to pass the examinations set for the 3 terms in secondary school to be able to move to the next class, and ace all your semesters at the university to help you maximize your journey, and fast track getting to your destination – graduation.

Some milestones might take longer to achieve than others, and depending on the route you plight to get there, be more effort and time consuming; yet, it doesn't make any milestone less critical than the other.

Journeying from Lagos to Anambra state of Nigeria by road is approximately 6h 38m drive and you will compulsorily pass through several states, and these states are indications of a new milestone. In-between these states, you will also pass some local governments marked by actual checkpoints with officers in uniform stopping to search vehicles as they journey, to ensure safety for all travellers.

When I embark on this journey, I watch out for milestones and checkpoints that serve as reminders of where I am, and how farther I am from where I'm coming from, and closer to where I am headed. Checkpoints might not be so obvious except I see signs, like barricades on the road, but I know I've hit a new milestone in my travel when I observe and see people with different cultures - dressings, languages, road structure, and mannerism generally.

As a younger person, you might be clueless about these things, and although this might be excusable for your younger mind, as you grow, your responsibilities increases, and time becomes a luxury, giving you more reasons why you cannot afford to just embark on journeys you are not able to measure, regardless of the sphere.

In a real life context, if the ultimate destination after defining what you want in your relationship/family sphere is to get married, have 4 children in the next 10 years, and finally relocate with your family, here are some key checklists:

- **Destination:** Your country of intended relocation.

- **Milestones:** Get married. Have the 1st child. Have the 2nd. Have the 3rd. Have the 4th. Raise enough relocation finances, etc.
- **Checkpoints:** Things you need to do to become desirable for marriage. Jobs/businesses to raise finances. Items to purchase to welcome your children, etc.

Note that there could be milestones in checkpoints, for instance, getting a new job is a checkpoint to raising enough finances, but it is also a milestone worth celebrating too. Got it?

Reflective Exercise:

It's your turn to test your understanding. Tom's desire in his career is to become the MD of the biggest bank in his country, in 20 years from today. Break this down for him:

- Destination: _______________________________
  ____
- Milestones: _______________________________
____
____
____
- Checkpoints: _______________________________
____
____
____
____

And, yes, you can have multiple destinations in a sphere of your life, these are what we call "options", and if you care to play safe, you need more than 3 options in every decision you make.

THE EDGE IN PREPARATION

There is that mistake of forgetting to prepare afresh for the next goal after achieving previous milestones. Recall that having it yesterday is not a guarantee you will have it tomorrow, except you are prepared enough for it.

A gift to an unprepared man is poison

Pause and reflect: Of what use is buying an oil perfume, opening it, and handing it over to a toddler to play with? Would it not be consumed in the absence of an adult? Is it not grossly unreasonable to appoint the post of the President of a nation to a teenager?

The next big thing – your next milestone is dependent on how prepared you are for it. When you have waited after achieving the first milestone in your journey, before you get frustrated about how long it is taking to record the next milestone, ask yourself how truly prepared you are. Nobody hands you over what you are actually not prepared to handle, mentally, emotionally, physically, and otherwise, according to the milestone you are pursuing.

A friend of mine shared a heart wrenching story with me about how a managing director in the company he used to work for was advised to resign. Prior to this day, he had been so devoted and actively building the hard skills he needed – bagged new degrees, professional certifications, memberships, and hands on experience. Guess what he failed to prepare for? The emotional intelligence needed to deal with each person's differences and uniqueness.

It is very great to prepare for the next job position by learning the hard skills you'd need, but never ignore the soft skills too. As you prepare to be financially stable enough to raise a family, don't neglect preparing your emotions for the stages and potential changes in the behavior of your spouse, or your children's potential need for closure.

Pay attention to everything you'd need to prepare for the next milestone, so, while you wait, keep preparing.

THE PLACE OF CELEBRATION

Why do you think there are graduation and convocation ceremonies? I love to believe it is the need to celebrate the milestone of having passed through school successfully, and aced all tests, regardless of the distractions.

Notice a reoccurring pattern of celebration in every concluded chapter of this book, purposed to remind you of the importance of celebrating any step you take – huge or little. Celebration is a catalyst to do more.

My HR experience gave me insights on numerous ways to keep your staff motivated on the job, one of which is to celebrate them when they perform considerably well. Organisations that take the time to celebrate their staff tend to get the most of them, than organisations that don't.

During a conversation with some friends that left their jobs, the most common reasons were the absence of recognition, overlooking of the targets they surpassed, and the constant focus and complaint of the minutest things they missed. While it is not advised to tie your source of motivation to whether you are celebrated on the job or not, it is human nature to crave being appreciated and celebrated.

It might not be a very big step, or a mighty ocean immediately, but every drop counts.

You can decide to make a habit of celebrating everything and anything that you do, and this celebration don't need to break your bank, it might also not cost you a dime either. Your object and method of celebration is solely up to you to decide.

There is no saner way to arrive at your destination than celebrating every time you achieve a milestone. Even as seemingly little as finally solving a mathematical equation that took you a longer time to solve, or accomplishing all the tasks you set out for a day, celebrate it!

AS YOU CELEBRATE...

Unleash your inner child

One of the reasons I enjoy watching kids play is that the moment they activate their play mood, they don't bother about anything at all, not even whether their caregivers or parents have enough money to pay the school fees for their next term. Isn't it beautiful to be able to switch off your busy button for a while?

Allow yourself become a child as you celebrate, no worries, no thoughts of the next thing to do, just you – with or without company, your box of chocolates, ice cream, new outfit, or your favorite playlist and dancing shoes!

Manage your energy

We are all beautifully wrapped boxes of energies, but are at will to decide whether the energies will be positive or negative. As you celebrate, feed on and be about the right energies and repel anything that gives the tinniest vibe of negativity.

The best ways to manage your energy are setting boundaries around them – what you'd take and what you won't, giving yourself time to rest in-between celebrations, knowing when to stop thinking about previous milestones, and start doing something about the next.

THE POWER OF GRATITUDE

I attended Ministers and Leaders Forum organized annually by Global Impact Ministries earlier in 2022, and one of the invited guests with several decades of leadership experience was asked how he overcame trials that kept coming in-between milestones, and his response "Be Grateful" was the highlight of that day for me.

We tend to think that achieving a new height exempts us from facing any further trial, but that is perhaps only in theory. I have come to realize that the easiest and most vulnerable time to get tempted is when you must have achieved a huge milestone. Ironic right? I know...

Yes, celebrate your milestones, but take heed as indicated in the chapter on live the moment, not to stay stuck on celebrating milestones you forget to go to the next new goal.

Amazingly, there is a power of gratitude that can break down walls that would try to build up during or after your milestone celebration, and even if these walls build up before you notice, sticking to gratitude is a positive energy that gives you solutions you wouldn't have seen if you stayed in that spot; blaming, grumbling or complaining.

It is impossible to go beyond a level you are grateful for

Do not also forget to be grateful for a milestone, even if it didn't come exactly as you expected it to come. As earlier mention in the chapter on stoppers, ingratitude has a way of stealing everything and belittling efforts, which in turn stops you from achieving any further goal or attaining any new height.

CHAPTER RECAP

10 key things to remember from this chapter

1. There is nothing like an unserious milestone because deciding to embark on your journey, set goals, take actions, and the refusal to back down regardless of oppositions, is worth the recognition.

2. Milestones are golden and cannot be disregarded, because not everyone who sets out on a journey ever smash the next goal, let alone arrives at their destinations.

3. Your destination is your end point; milestones mark the completion of a goal, and checkpoints are in-between milestones to help decide your fit for a new milestone.

4. Milestones and checkpoints are reminders of where you are, how farther you are from where you came from, and how close you are to where you're headed.

5. No one gives you what you are unprepared for. Your next milestone is dependent on how well you are prepared for it.

6. Don't prepare in an aspect, and ignore the rest. What you don't prepare for can sabotage what you prepared for.

7. Celebrate every milestone no matter how seemingly little. It serves as a catalyst that spurs you to do even more.

8. The method of celebration is yours to decide, but quit thinking you have to do so much to celebrate. It could

be a box of chocolate or learning a new dance move with one thing in mind, "celebrate!"

9. As you celebrate, unleash your inner child, and manage your energy.

10. It is impossible to go beyond a level you are grateful for. Being grateful for the next milestone fast tracks it.

CHAPTER EXERCISE

Complete this in your personal journal.

Observe all you really want in various spheres of your life according to the chapter 1 of this book, now rewrite your destination per sphere, jot down your milestones, and finally decide your checkpoints.

Across each milestone, write out the ways you will celebrate, as you attain them. Would it be a box of chocolate or a new item? It could be anything that makes you happy – little or much.

Your Special Treat!

After you complete this chapter, including the reflection and exercises, celebrate with one of the items you have listed above! Hooray! Cheers to your amazing progress!

REPEAT PERFORMANCE

"Average minds analyse. Great minds execute"

— Lewis Howes.

There are a lot of people in the world struggling to attain the exact success you are striving to attain, so, although the sky is big enough for everyone to fly freely, there is always that hassle to attain success as fast as you can – this is common human nature.

You need to understand that saying "I want this success" is not a good enough reason why success should automatically be handled over to you, neither is saying "I have read this book" enough to translate into a life of authenticity, satisfaction or off stuck points. If wishes were horses... well, they are not. The question is: what miles are you willing to go to get it all?

When you buy a product you expect to give you a particular result as was described by the honest manufacturer, you don't use it one day and it automatically works. You'd need to repeat its' usage, as oft as you want a sustained result. And when repeating the usage, you have to be sure there are no contradictory products you're using that is capable of sabotaging the process, or stifle the ability of the product to serve its' designed purpose.

This means that it is one thing to have all the principles spelt out in this book and other world bestselling self-help or mentoring books at your immediate disposal, it is yet another to actually practice all that is instructed in continuum, to get actual and evident results.

The ultimate victory is in continuous repetition of processes, and revamping as would be required. While in the process, you are aware of those things that have the capacity to sabotage your efforts *(Check chapter on stoppers again),* and you are consciously addressing them. Be mindful that when your victory starts coming, you don't self sabotage it thinking it came too easily, or that you don't deserve it, because you absolutely do. You didn't come this far, to just come this far!

A BURNING DESIRE TO WIN OR WIN

The secret to repeating a performance enough to get your proposed result is rooted in your burning desire to win or win; no grey areas. A burning desire is simply how "passionately" you want a thing to happen for you; and until you have that crave or yearn that make you refuse to give up or give in, that dream might not happen.

From where I come from, not every big brand wants to associate themselves with activities of startups, whereas this is largely advised from a research I carried out for my MBA thesis – collaborative ideation and organisational performance, because of the opportunity to improve impact and innovation. Yet, a friend of mine didn't care...

Even with an understanding of this, this friend I met during my volunteering days in 2015 spoke to me about an amazing project she was putting together to help up and coming entertainers, and the need to penetrate either of the big brands for sponsorships. Anyone who heard her would have tagged her crazy, but then, "craziness" in dreaming is what a burning desire really is about.

She shared her ideas and we proceeded to creating an excellent proposal and documents to present to the big brands for sponsorship. What got me so motivated was how she dedicated so much time to writing to select brands I wouldn't have imagined she'd have dared to, and even when they wouldn't get back, her follow-up was second to none.

A burning desire gives you all the guts you need

Well, her program was live and a recorded success in October 2021 and I am even looking forward to a successful 2nd edition in 2022.

The desire was indeed burning!

When you want something desperately, not to the extreme of doing anything negative to get it, but with a positive outlook, you will go for it like that's all the option you've got ...burn all bridges behind and leaving yourself no possible way to retreat, you'd understand that you can only hit hard... no recoil and no regrets!

But, hey, no futile journeys, a burning desire could also mean looking for other ways to get things done, the whole idea is to "get it done" relentlessly.

DISCIPLINE FOR THE TIMES YOU DON'T FEEL LIKE IT

If we would address this with all honesty, we'd agree that you are not always inspired to see through on tasks, none of us really are. We were all built with the power of will – the power to decide what we want to do, and at what time we want to. But if we continually misuse this power, getting positive results are unlikely.

It is normal to feel the need to stay in bed for longer hours, procrastinate tasks to a more "convenient" time, make an excuse for not starting that project, give solid reasons for not spending time with your family and Significant other, or simply not do anything about a situation that don't seem too easy or pleasant.

Candidly, there'd always be a reason not to do what you should, but if you succumb to that reason, you succumb to continued dissatisfaction. No one really wants that, you shouldn't ever.

When your zeal fails you, discipline will keep you.

You need to come to an understanding that you don't get things done because you want to, or because it is convenient, but because you have to, and that the present and future outcomes depend on it. Discipline is commanding yourself to do a thing even when you don't feel like doing it, discipline is the real self-control.

When I started writing this book, I had so many reasons not to complete it within my set time frame, and if I decide to write all the reasons now, you'd definitely support me. As a matter of fact, before I forced myself into being disciplined, I had procrastinated for a whole year. So, you see, it hits us all and there is absolutely nothing wrong with you.

You just need to develop discipline and be consistent about what you have to do, and here are ways to:

Don't overestimate your strengths, don't underestimate your weaknesses

Discipline doesn't mean pushing for what you know isn't yours to do, in comparison to your strength. Even if you spend the entire time trying to stay disciplined on a project you start, it might be futile if you are not doing it in line with your strengths.

There are things you do with ease and with lesser stress than other people around you - your strength, when you focus on those things; it is less likely that discipline will be difficult. In the same light, there are things you know you are not good at - your weaknesses, while you try to work on those weaknesses, be sure not to act like they don't exist.

Start small

Sometimes, it is not as though you actually lack discipline or that you are lazy, it is just that you want to do everything at the same time, or even rush the process. That tires you out before you even try!

Perhaps you want to switch your career from being an accountant to being a nurse, if you do not take the time to take one course at a time; you will become bombarded with courses and tasks, which automatically cripple your mind from even starting at all, or seeing through on what you've already started.

I know you want to become the Governor of your state soon, but if you'd ever become, you'd need to start from taking baby steps, pace perfect *(Refer to chapter on find your pace),* and scale up progressively.

When you start small, it is easier to build discipline simply because you are less preoccupied with tasks or pressure.

Belittle temptations

Temptations might not be completely avoidable, but can be made irrelevant or belittled.

At a less enlightened point in my life, I had terrible phone habits. For once, when I woke up, the first thing I'd do is fiddle with my phone, as I believe most people do. Some other times, I might be working on my phone, but constantly responding to beeps and notifications from my social media accounts, even my email. It took me a while to recognize how this hindered the effective utilization of my 24 hours.

The prior intention when you pick your phone up in the morning might be to check your emails or do something productive, and coincidentally, a social media notification pops up and you decide to check it out. . . You are tempted to have a quick check on other media accounts, on and on, and hours are spent doing nothing meaningful.

If you know your most common source of temptation, find a way to lose its' grip. For me, it used to be my phone. What is it for you?

Remind yourself why you started in the first instance

Discipline is easier to build when you can remind yourself the big enough reason why you started.

What was the idea behind you taking that course? Was it to build your skills, get promotions, land a new job opportunity, or just maintain relevance? Whatever you do, always remember why you started doing it in the first place. This helps your mind hold on to tangible reasons you will need to achieve all your set goals.

Don't wait for approvals

One of the mistakes we make is tying our performance and next step to the approval of people. If you live by this, it will be impossible to be disciplined enough to achieve a thing simply because you're waiting for others to give you a thumbs up on every achievement.

If you will build discipline, you'd need to learn how to applaud yourself for a job well done. Everyone is constantly striving to become a success, and if you will join the moving train, you'd need to discipline yourself to keep going outside the influences of others, and that's whether they approve of you or not.

Create rituals and habits

When you discover a habit that is hindering you from achieving what you need to, building discipline will require you to create a counter habit or ritual.

With regards to my phone habit, I made a choice to keep it far from me before I sleep, so it is not the first thing I see when I wake. Then I proceeded to setting an alarm for major activities I wanted to repeat during the course of the day. I have alarms that reminds me to read my affirmations, pray, post on social media, pause work to get breathers, switch between tasks, get my lunch break, end the break, read a chapter, meditate, plan the next day, practice gratitude, etc. I also have special days with special alarms for tasks that are less frequent.

These rituals can be the minutest things that matter; it could go on and on until you begin to do it without over processing it, because you have consciously impressed it in your subconscious mind.

HABITS AND LIFESTYLES – THE 21/90 RULE

The 21/90 rule became a thing in 1960, introduced by Dr. Maxwell Maltz. This rule states that it takes 21 days to form a habit and 90 days to make it a lifestyle. This means that if you have a thing to change about yourself – good or bad, if you keep doing the opposite for about 21 consecutive days, you'd form a new habit, and if you keep that up for 90 days, it can become a part of you – a lifestyle. How possible is this?

Pause and reflect: Why do you think that after plighting a route for a long time, even when your mind is busy or absent, you can still navigate your way without any one guiding you through? Habits and lifestyles...

My reading habit wasn't great at a point in my life; it was so terrible that after my volunteering that ended in 2016, out of the 5 amazing books I was gifted, only one got read in 2016, the rest had to wait until 2020. I knew something was missing in me but I couldn't figure it out at the time, I mean who would have guessed reading would have helped?

One day during a program I attended, the speaker shared words of wisdom that birthed a reader in me, "The "you" today is the "you" there'd be tomorrow, the only difference will be the people you meet and the books you read". Well, I started small, and scaled up progressively. What habits do you need to build now?

AS YOU PERFORM...

Give yourself a big enough reason why

What is your greatest motivation? Why do you really want to succeed? Why do you want to overcome stagnation? Why do you want to experience a deep level of satisfaction?

When it looks like you've gotten an answer each, you still need to keep asking yourself "why", until you get the root trigger.

From the outlook, you might say you want to get a new career because that's where the world is going, but repeatedly asking yourself "why" might open your heart to understand you probably want to have financial freedom, or breakout of the poverty that hindered your caregivers; it could be anything at all that might not be grasped immediately.

When you get that big enough reason why, it solidifies your driving force to perform, and chase your goals in consistency.

Reinforce your why

Reinforcement is a boosting factor that strengthens the "big why" you have discovered, it could be positive or negative reinforcement, highlighted below:

- Positive reinforcement: Here, you give yourself positive reasons to get things done. Example, if I complete this tasks and repeat my performance, I can gradually change the trajectory of my life, overcome stagnation, and finally attain the success my caregivers couldn't.

- Negative reinforcement: Here, you remind yourself of the negative effect of not getting these things done.

Example: if I don't get this done now, I might never overcome stagnation, or attain success, and that's an automatic entrance to poverty.

Sincerely, both will work, but here's what a long run of applying either of them looks like:

- Positive reinforcement gives you the feel good emotions while you go through your journey.

- Negative reinforcement might work in the short run, but the long run will be filled with anxiety that end up distorting the entire journey.

Remain calm

The calmer your mind, the more productive you become and the greater your outcome. Calmness of mind is one of the greatest gifts of life. In fact, it is a personal victory when you can finally control, and quiet your mind in the most turbulent times.

As you repeat performance of stipulated reflections, maintain a calm state of mind, identify your sources of turbulence, address them, and stay away from its' triggers – things, topics, and people.

A calmer you is one capable of breaking forth with ideas and productively getting things done to achieve success. You have to break the cycle of turbulence to regain your power.

Act the part

Envision your highest self, and begin this day to show up as such. Not given to fakery, but a conscious awareness of self, genuine acceptance of the vision, and an unwavering commitment to becoming that part you play.

Act the part until you get the part.

A life can be shaped in so many ways, one of which is choosing to act in accordance to that highest self you have envisioned. At this stage, you begin to activate the powers so hidden inside of you.

If you want to become a business owner in 5 years, start acting like a business owner will act. If you wish to be a parent, start acting like a parent would. This will affect the way you speak, coordinate yourself, and manage your emotions, even as little as the way you walk would have to be affected too.

Among the many other things this will do for you, it will help you control the limit you have placed on your mind about how far you can actually get, help you cut down on habits that don't align with your highest self, sharpen your understanding of what the future holds for you, teach you the steps you will need to take each day to get closer, and finally, attract the right kind of people you'd need in your life as you perform.

Maintain the spirit of excellence

Have you been privileged to review CVs and resumes? If yes, then you'd understand how loosely the word "excellence" is now being used. I could almost bet that people use it because it looks fanciful, and not for the actuality of its' meaning. You see people writing "I am excellence driven" on their personal summary, until it is time to execute a task when no one is there to guide, instruct, or monitor them, and they are back to doing other things outside their job jurisdiction.

Excellence is your ability to perform your duties and responsibilities when no one is watching, when no one is there to applaud you, to give you a pat on the back, or monitor you to ensure you carry out all that's yours to do.

As you perform, maintain the spirit of excellence. Do it for you, do it to overcome stagnation, do it for your future, do it for a life of prolonged satisfaction, and nothing short of that.

THE EVIDENCE, NOT THE JOURNEY

Was that an error? No, it's wasn't. As you perform, bear in mind that while your concern is your journey, and how to achieve all you are capable of, a greater percentage of people around you will only care about your evidences. Is this fair? No! Can this change? Well, I really can't guarantee a yes.

You need to master the act of never depending on anyone's interest in your journey, and refuse to feel bad when hardly anyone shows up to pledge their support, especially when you just begin, and more so when your dreams are crazy, and unfathomable by the common man.

The evidence, not the journey! The progress, not the process! Be serious about your efforts, people care only about the results.

The amount of seriousness placed on yourself determines your outcome. Paying serious attention to yourself will cut across your health routines, purpose navigations, mindset adjustments, circle selections, diligence in little, persistence after a fall, consistence in moving, and everything that makes up your journey to satisfaction.

Essentially, as you focus on the few that support, always remember it is solely your responsibility to do more for yourself, and produce those evidences for you alone!

WIN!

CHAPTER RECAP

10 key things to remember from this chapter

1. Saying you want to be successful is not enough reason why success should be handed over to you, what miles are you willing to go to get it?
2. Like you'd repeat the use of a product to get the best of it, repeating a performance can give you similar result.
3. Develop the desire to either win or win, no grey areas.
4. You won't always feel like repeating a performance, but discipline will help you. Discipline is commanding yourself to do a thing when you don't feel like doing it.
5. To help you boost discipline, start small, never overestimate your strength or underestimate your weaknesses, belittle present and potential distractions, remind yourself why you started out in the first instance, don't wait for approvals, create healthy habits.
6. The 21/90 rule states that if you do a thing consistently for 21 days, you will form a habit, and when you go as far as 90 days, you develop a lifestyle.
7. As you repeat your performance, give yourself a big enough reason why, reinforce your why, remain calm, act the part, and maintain the spirit of excellence.
8. Positive reinforcement helps you feel good as you journey, negative reinforcement might work in the short run, but the long run will be filled with anxiety.
9. Envision your highest self, and begin to show up as that.
10. Be serious about your efforts, people care only about the results.

CHAPTER EXERCISE

Complete this in your personal journal.

What habits do you think has played a huge role in stopping you? Like the solution to my phone habits, what counter habits would you need to inculcate?

In building discipline, I wrote "Chinwe, no more excuses!" on my ceiling, right above my bed, so it's the first thing I see once I open my eyes. It has really helped. . . So, write a simple sentence with a command to yourself. It could be in a piece of paper, but put it somewhere you'd always see it. And, hey, be mindful not to look the other way when you see it.

Lastly, why do you want all you've been striving for? What is your big enough reason why? Probe yourself continuously, until you address the "core" reason why.

Your Special Treat!

After you complete this chapter, including the reflection and exercises, do something you've always wanted to do, but find yourself procrastinating! Bravo! I celebrate your progress with you!

CONCLUSION

"The expectations of life depend upon diligence; the mechanic that would perfect his work must first sharpen his tools."

— Confucius.

I am the most glad that you made thus far, hats off!

It is an already established fact that I play a lot, and on one of those days, I learned the following helpful lessons on a hockey table which will be beneficial as you execute and reignite your journey to a life of satisfaction:

The dedication to win

I got into the game with one goal – win it! In the real sense, is that not why you read this book? Is that not why we are all striving daily? We long for an eventual win, the victory of finally identifying our core reason of creation – purpose, setting and achieving goals, creating ideas and executing them, impacting on lives, building successful relationships, raising morally solid families... literally, a 360 degree win.

Unwavering focus

When you set your mind up for a win, you need to FOCUS. You cannot afford to leave life to chances; you need to stay determined, never given to distractions – anger, pride, social media, excuses, etc. Nothing else should matter to us more than winning.

Strategy design

While playing, I had to think out a comeback strategy

because I had lost the first round. Sometimes, the first round or first shot at life might not be the winning shot, would you then quit? No, No and No. At this point you revamp on what next to do. How do you intend to accomplish these wins? What will you need to put in place? After a fall, what would you need to do differently?

Take advantage of opportunities

All I needed was a slip from my opponent to drive my ball to win, a slip I wouldn't have recognized if I didn't stubbornly refuse to accept defeat. In real life scenario, opportunities will always burst forth; you need to constantly be at alert for them. As you stay at alert, keep preparing yourself to take absolute advantage of all.

Victory at last

I had a different kind of dance step when I eventually won, and that will be your story too. You will win, I tell you, you will. You've just got to do what you've got to do!

--

At the end of the day, you need to be able to comfortably say you utilized every tool that was given to you - every gifts, talents, skills, this book, everything; it is that or nothing at all.

You are never stranded!

Your tools are in your hands, have always been the whole time. This book was designed to trigger it, as I hope it has been able to. You do, you have all you need to live that life you desire, here and now, for there's nothing like being stranded in destiny. The major problems are in the way we focus on what others have, belittle what we have, and the refusal to upbeat what we have to remain relevant based on the world's adjustments.

Life is like a giant Rubik cube, you'd need to keep twisting it until you get the right combinations. To make sense out of life, no one strategy will give you a lasting result, you need to understand the principles of different combinations, you need to REVAMP!

- Keep twisting.
- Try everything you think you can.
- Take a shot at all ideas that come to you.
- Come alive!

What do you have? Do something with them and live the most fulfilled and satisfied life.

It is my deepest pleasure to be a part of your unique journey, here's the next steps to take if this book was helpful, and you'd need me to be your accountability partner, or share in your successes and victories:

Send an email to: chinweebere2022@gmail.com

Other contacts: https://linktr.ee/chinweandro

BIOGRAPHY

Chinwe Ebere A. (The Impacter) is a Social Entrepreneur, Founder, Master Life Coach and Consultant at Andromagik Company – A Social Enterprise and an Expressionism Brand.

Chinwe is interested in the 360 degree wholeness of individuals and teams. She believes everyone possesses immeasurable potentials, as such; she is able to trigger the conscious and consistent efforts to help you become the best version of yourself, by digging deep for answers, identifying potential stoppers, and creatively converting negative and positive energies into endless possibilities.

Chinwe's day to day efforts is on identifying institutional voids and collaboratively creating the most innovative solutions to prevailing global issues, some to commence in the coming years. Her commitments focus on individual's mental well-being, quality education, zero poverty, and collaborative ideation, to not only create impacts but raise a tribe of impacters for a wider influence.

She has a Bachelor degree in Industrial Relations and Personnel Management from the University of Lagos; a Master Life Coach Certification from Transformation Academy, USA and Master of Business Administration (MBA) Management, from the University of Lagos. She is a Certified Strategist with the International Strategic Management Institute (ISMI), and a Member of the

Chartered Institute of Personnel Management (CIPM) – Certified body governing the activities of Human Resources in Nigeria. She is a Certified Mental Health Ambassador.

Chinwe actively speaks on impact, purpose discovery and navigation, harnessing potentials, improving mental health, finding happiness, building confidence and esteem, setting and achieving goals. She currently hosts a Youtube series "A Quick Stop with Chinwe Andro" on her page "Chinwe Andro", where she shares practicable life tips and wisdom nuggets.

Chinwe's experience is versatile, as she has track record of success in B2B and B2C communications, HR and administrative management, business management, startup consulting, training and program management, customer experience and innovation management. With this, she is able to set organisations up for sustained success.

Chinwe's joy is derived from ideating, speaking, writing, reading, networking, and creative problem solving.